IDA KAR

IDA KAR
BOHEMIAN PHOTOGRAPHER

IDA KAR
BOHEMIAN PHOTOGRAPHER

CLARE FREESTONE
KAREN WRIGHT

National Portrait Gallery, London

Published in Great Britain by National Portrait Gallery Publications,
National Portrait Gallery, St Martin's Place, London, WC2H 0HE

Published to accompany the exhibition *Ida Kar: Bohemian Photographer, 1908–1974*
at the National Portrait Gallery, London from 10 March to 19 June 2011.

For a complete catalogue of current publications please write to the
address above, or visit our website at www.npg.org.uk/publications

ISBN 978 1 85514 422 4

A catalogue record for this book is available from the British Library.

10 9 8 7 6 5 4 3 2 1

Head of Publications: Celia Joicey
Managing Editor: Christopher Tinker
Project Editor: Robert Davies
Production Manager: Ruth Müller-Wirth
Design: Price Watkins

Printed in China.

Endpapers: Ida Kar, pencil and ink drawing by S. Stepanian, 1957
Frontispiece: Ida Kar, self-portrait with sculptures by Brian Robins, 1955
Pages 10–11: Whitechapel Art Gallery installation, March 1960
Pages 56–7: Jacob Epstein's studio, including the sculptures
Social Consciousness and *Ecce Homo*, 1953

CONTENTS

6

Gallery One window, 1954

8

Ida Kar photographing Sir Charles Wheeler,
by John Cox, 1960

FOREWORD
SANDY NAIRNE
DIRECTOR, NATIONAL PORTRAIT GALLERY

IN 1960 a major exhibition of Ida Kar's photographs was presented at the Whitechapel Art Gallery – an important statement about her work and about photography as a significant contemporary art form. Rather than viewing photography as part of the media world, or as something merely of documentary interest, an influential public gallery was making a positive critical comment. This acknowledgement of Kar's work was taken a stage further when, in 1989, Val Williams' monographic study was published by Virago Press. In 1981 the National Portrait Gallery made its first acquisition of photographs by Kar – twenty vintage prints – and two decades later purchased the Ida Kar archive, which includes more than 800 prints and some 10,000 negatives. This exhibition will achieve, we hope, a wider appreciation of Kar's work, and adds to a sequence of exhibitions of outstanding women photographers from Julia Margaret Cameron and Lee Miller to Annie Leibovitz.

Ida Kar was born to Armenian parents living in Russia and spent her early working life as an artist in Paris and Cairo, before she arrived in London in 1945. Here she formed friendships and working relationships as part of the burgeoning post-war artistic community, most importantly with the critic and gallery-owner Victor Musgrave, who became her second husband. Her emergence as a photographer was linked to creating images of writers and artists pictured in their working environments. If she was part of a bohemian world – an idea stretching back to Henri Murger's *Scenes of Bohemian Life* through Giacomo Puccini's *La Bohème* and novels such as George du Maurier's *Trilby* and Joyce Cary's *The Horse's Mouth* – it was the base for making the most telling and sympathetic portraits.

I am very grateful to Clare Freestone for curating the exhibition with the particular support of Terence Pepper and Georgia Atienza, Karen Wright for contributing an essay, Rosie Wilson for managing the exhibition, and Robert Davies for project-editing this catalogue. Special thanks are also due to the other members of the Photographs Department, as well as to Sarah Tinsley, Celia Joicey and Christopher Tinker. There are many others at the Gallery I should also thank, including Michael Barrett, Pim Baxter, Andrea Easey, Neil Evans, Ian Gardner, Michelle Greaves, Justine McLisky, Ruth Müller-Wirth, Doris Pearce, Sabina Rahman, Jude Simmons and Helen Whiteoak.

ESSAYS

Self-portrait, late 1950s

ARTIST WITH A CAMERA
CLARE FREESTONE

IT IS 22 MARCH 1960, three months into a new decade. The Whitechapel Art Gallery, celebrated for director Bryan Robertson's dynamic exhibition programme, is holding its first major photographic exhibition – a retrospective of the work of Ida Kar. The 300 guests enjoying caviar and champagne at the opening are unlikely to have seen many photographs in the gallery before, and certainly not a whole show devoted to a photographer, a female one at that, for this is the first solo photographic show to be held at a major London art gallery. The most established of Britain's photographers, Cecil Beaton, is among the guests and is admiring Kar's portrait of himself. The photograph is enlarged on a grand scale, more than three feet square, and hung within a carefully planned dynamic installation of more than 100 works. Kar's fellow Armenian, the businessman and socialite Nubar Gulbenkian, is moving through the crowd, and one of Kar's sitters, the glamorous actress Mai Zetterling, wearing a 'gleaming red mackintosh',[1] embodies the allure of the occasion.

Fifty years after this event, the National Portrait Gallery is presenting a reevaluation of the work of one of the key figures of twentieth-century portraiture. Despite receiving public and critical acclaim from her contemporaries, Ida Kar remains surprisingly little known. She worked among avant-garde writers and artists from diverse disciplines and, as a documentary portraitist, her photographs provide an extraordinary insight into post-war cultural life.

FORMATIVE YEARS

Ida Kar was born Ida Karamian in the city of Tambov, 400km south-east of Moscow, on 8 April 1908, the only daughter of Armenian parents. In Yerevan (at the time called Erevan), the Armenian capital, Kar's parents lived close to the university, where her father, Melkon, taught French and Persian while her mother cared for the family. The Karamians moved to the Egyptian city of Alexandria in 1921, where Melkon continued to teach and Ida was educated at the prestigious Lycée Français.

In 1928 Kar, encouraged by her father, studied medicine and chemistry in Paris, but shortly after her arrival decided to pursue singing and violin lessons instead. Four years earlier the first surrealist manifesto had been published in the city, which was a thriving artistic centre. Kar settled among the bohemian residents of the Left Bank and became acquainted with Suzanne Dechevaux-Dumesnil, a skilled pianist who would later marry Samuel Beckett. She introduced Kar to Heinrich Heidersberger, a young German surrealist painter and photographer

Ida Kar, 1934

Heinrich Heidersberger, self-portrait, 1930

Muhammad Ali Mosque, Cairo, 1943

who had been drawn to Paris as the centre of surrealism. That movement would come to inspire Kar's early non-portrait photographs, of which no examples are known to survive. At Heidersberger's studio on Rue Perrier, in the Paris suburb of Montrouge, Kar assisted in photographic experiments using a rudimentary wooden camera. Together they attended the premiere of Buñuel and Dalí's film *Un chien andalou* and a screening of Eisenstein's *Battleship Potemkin*. Their friends included the Dutch-born artists Gerard Hordyk and Piet Mondrian and the French surrealist painter Yves Tanguy.

In 1933 Kar returned to the family home in Alexandria, where, working as a photographer's assistant, she met and married Edmond Belali, a government official and keen amateur photographer. On moving to Cairo, they opened a studio called Idabel (combining their names), which operated from a fashionable quarter and specialised in dramatically lit, closely cropped portraits and surrealistic still lifes.

Cairo had an active surrealist group, centred on the poet Georges Henein and his partner Ikbal El Alailly. Kar became a member of the group, meeting at Tommy's Bar and showing Idabel's work in the *Art and Freedom* exhibitions held in 1943 and 1944. Among those collaborating with the surrealist group as a poet and artist was Victor Musgrave (pp.46, 48), a young English Royal Air Force officer stationed in Cairo who edited the services periodical *Contact* and wrote art criticism for the *Egyptian Gazette*. Meeting Musgrave changed the path of Kar's life; during the War, Kar and Belali were divorced to allow for her marriage to Musgrave in 1944. Their home in Darb el-Labana was visited by many international writers and artists, creating a lively and intellectual social scene.

LONDON

In 1945 the newly-weds moved to London, taking up residence in a small flat at 34b Devonshire Close, W1, close to Regent's Park. As the art critic Jasia Reichardt later commented, Kar's 'early years in England could have been plotted on a chart with the following headings: perseverance, blundering, despair, hope, frustration'.[2] She was, nevertheless, resourceful enough to mount two exhibitions of her work in the 1940s. In 1946 Kar arranged with Olwen Vaughan, the former secretary of the British Film Institute, to show her work at the New London Film Society, and in May 1947 she exhibited alongside the sculptor Robert Couturier at the Anglo-French Art Centre in St John's Wood.

Photography exhibitions in London were uncommon, and continued to be so throughout the 1950s. In 1952 Kar visited the first exhibition in London of the work of Henri Cartier-Bresson, held at the Institute of Contemporary Arts (ICA), which had been founded ten years earlier. *Photographs by Henri Cartier-Bresson* was enthusiastically received: 'photography was debated in front of a packed house ... by which time it had also become an important topic at the Slade School of Fine Art.'[3]

To make a living, Kar turned her attention to theatrical photography and in 1947 began to advertise for commissions. For a fee of two guineas (equivalent to about £50 today) the sitter obtained five proofs of different positions and one

John Christoforou, 1953

Bill Hopkins, 1955

15

finished glossy 10 x 8-inch print. Kar's 'portrait heads', taken with a Sanderson plate camera and dramatically lit using two Photoflood lamps, appeared in the actors' casting directory *Spotlight*. She made her prints in a darkroom at 61 Seymour Street, near the Edgware Road, rented from her friend the literary photographer Mark Gerson.

It took Kar some time after moving to London to remodel the artistic and literary social scene she had enjoyed with Musgrave in Egypt. She first encountered the London art world in the late 1940s, when she and Musgrave moved to a building at 1 Litchfield Street, just off Charing Cross Road, where the painter John Christoforou (above) had established a small gallery. In 1953, on Christoforou's departure to France, Musgrave reopened the space as 'Gallery One' with initial capital of just £5, while Kar's studio was established on a floor above. Gallery One was soon fêted for showing art from outside the mainstream, with an impressive programme that included the first solo shows of F.N. Souza (1955) and Gillian Ayres (1956) and London's first exhibitions of Enrico Baj's nuclear paintings (1957) and Yves Klein's monochromes (1957).

The writer Bill Hopkins (left), who was associated with the group of playwrights and novelists known as the 'Angry Young Men', became a lodger at Litchfield Street in 1954 and recalls a residence on the edge of Soho where authors and painters mixed with socialites and the *demi-monde*.[4] The Kar-Musgrave household was a meeting point for bohemians; Kar's companions included the artist Brian Robins (p.16), who in the early 1950s worked nearby as one of the last lamplighters in London. Kar's contact sheets and negatives trace a long

friendship; they contain portraits of the young Robins, his marriage to Susan, nude studies and images of The Farm, the coffee shop that Robins opened with his wife in 1959 to 'show works of art and sell coffee' (p.131).[5]

Kar's introduction to Jacob Epstein gave her access to several of the sculptor's sitters, including Somerset Maugham (p.115), Gina Lollobrigida and Anna Neagle. In the early 1950s Kar assisted in the guardianship of Epstein's son, the painter Theodore Garman, who suffered from a mental illness. She travelled with Garman to Italy shortly before his untimely death in 1954. Kar's photographs of Epstein at work in his studio include her study of Epstein sculpting a bust of Bertrand Russell. She used this as her 1953 Christmas card and it was one of the first of her portraits to be syndicated by the photographic agency Camera Press (p.143).

Founded by Tom Blau in 1947, Camera Press represented the Armenian-born portraitist Yousuf Karsh, as well as Kar's contemporary rivals Baron and Jane Bown, and from 1953 the agency syndicated Kar's images worldwide. Records show that her portraits were distributed to the Netherlands, South Africa, Australia and Finland, while the *Jewish Chronicle* and *Yorkshire Post* were among British clients itemised on a later sales report.[6]

FORTY ARTISTS FROM LONDON AND PARIS

From left sitters include: **Ann Secord;
Ida Kar; Lynn Chadwick,** 1954

The year 1954 was one of great creative activity. In assembling an impressive catalogue of sitters Kar spent a weekend photographing Lynn Chadwick (left) and his family at Pinswell in Cheltenham, and began a friendship with Ivon and Mollie Hitchens, whom she photographed for the first time at home in Petworth, Essex. She photographed John Piper at Fawley Bottom Farmhouse in Henley and Reg Butler in his Berkhamsted studio (he thought the results of the shoot 'Splendid'[7]). Kenneth Armitage requested a print of his portrait for use in a British Council catalogue, and Kar photographed L.S. Lowry at a Whitechapel Art Gallery exhibition.

Kar travelled to Paris in the spring and made a 'busy round of visits to studios and ateliers', organising sittings with what Bill Hopkins termed 'rebels mellowed by the popular appreciation they have discovered in middle age'.[8] The resulting portraits, including those of the artists Le Corbusier, Alberto Giacometti (below), Marie Laurencin, Joan Miró, Germaine Richier and Ossip Zadkine, appeared in Gallery One on 12 October as *Forty Artists from London and Paris* (pp.62–79). The show lasted three weeks and received positive press coverage. *Art News and Review* reported, 'This is a fascinating and entertaining show, and if so many creative faces, exposed within such modest confines, leave the visitor slightly fatigued, it can only be counted a tribute to Miss Kar's unerring gift for extracting so much of her subjects' personality.'[9]

17

Alberto Giacometti, page from Kar's Artists album, Paris, 1954

18

ARTISTS AND WRITERS IN LONDON

Twenty-one-year-old John Kasmin, who had recently returned to London from New Zealand, was immediately attracted to the Gallery One scene. From 1956 to 1958 he was Kar's assistant and worked for Musgrave at Gallery One. Kasmin subscribed to the typescript publication *Celebrity Service*, which announced the arrival of public figures to London, and brought potential sitters to Kar's attention. Kasmin would suggest to the sitters, such as Raymond Chandler and the Australian painter Sidney Nolan, that Kar was working to commission, then try to place the portraits with the press. After two years the arrangement was formalised; in a contractual letter, Kar asked Kasmin to be her 'manager and sole representative of [her] work', in which role he continued until the early 1960s.[10] Kasmin had an acute business sense – he went on to open his own gallery in 1963, and later became a prominent international art dealer. He worked hard at promoting Kar and organised

Vijaya Lakshmi Pandit, 1958

high-profile sittings, such as those with T.S. Eliot at the Faber & Faber offices, future Poet Laureate Cecil Day-Lewis, the sculptor Elisabeth Frink and the playwright Noël Coward at the Dorchester Hotel (opposite). Kasmin sold Kar's unlikely photograph of the President of the Royal Academy, Sir Charles Wheeler, sliding down a banister, to the *Daily Express* for £50 – the most he obtained for a single image.

In March 1956 Gallery One reopened in larger premises in Soho. *Vogue* reported that 'People are talking about an interesting new gallery at 20 D'Arblay Street, W1, run by Victor Musgrave (winner of the Soho Festival Poetry Prize last summer). His wife, Ida Kar, a photographer with an extraordinary and tender talent for portrait work, also has a studio there.'[11] This move brought Kar and Musgrave into the heart of London bohemia, where the 'misfit' writer Colin MacInnes had also gravitated. MacInnes later noted that 'there nobody fitted – that was the point'.[12] MacInnes took a room in the D'Arblay Street building early in 1956. 'I soon discovered Victor was, like myself, a noctambule,' he said, 'and we would often walk at night round Soho or Mayfair.'[13] MacInnes introduced his young friend the painter and writer Terry Taylor to Kar, and within a week Taylor (below) had moved in as her assistant. He remembers, 'Ida was a skilled cook and we would all sit at the table at least a couple of times a day. There would be Victor, maybe Kasmin, a visiting artist, sometimes Colin MacInnes, myself, visiting friends.'[14] Multilingual and with an international background, Kar loved conversing, but was 'not a mad social animal and didn't drink a lot of alcohol or take drugs at all. She attended many cultural events, visited friends, gallery openings and the odd club. The Colony Room was her favourite.'[15]

The growing multiculturalism found within London was embraced by Kar and Musgrave. Gallery One's exhibitors ranged from Yugoslav painter Zlatko Prica in 1957 to *Seven Indian Painters in Europe* in 1958, which was opened by Indian High Commissioner Vijaya Lakshmi Pandit (left). The gallery represented Sudanese-born artist Hussein Shariffe and Indian-born painter F.N. Souza, whose careers Musgrave did much to promote. As well as photographing these artists, Kar portrayed Trinidadian-born writer Samuel Selvon at the time of the publication of his novel *The Lonely Londoners* (1956), which considered contemporary notions of ethnicity by detailing the lives of a number of West Indian immigrants.

Self-portrait with Terry Taylor, 1956

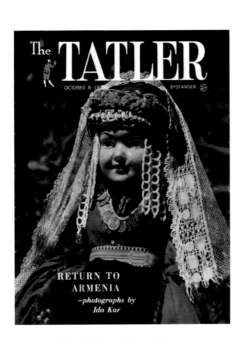

DOCUMENTARY PORTRAITS

Working to commission, Kar travelled to Armenia in 1957 for the first time since her childhood. She visited her ageing parents and a photograph she made of her father on this occasion became one of her favourite portraits (below). Her treatment as an honoured guest increased her self-confidence, as did sittings with artists including the sculptor Nikogos Nikogosyan, and an exhibition of her Armenian photographs in the capital Yerevan (Erevan) in August. The photographs published in 'Return to Armenia', a feature in the *Tatler & Bystander* on 8 October 1958 documenting Kar's interest in both the traditions and contemporary culture of the country, include a portrait of the architect G. Aghabian and a striking image of a girl in national costume. In spring 1958 Kar was travelling again; this time to Moscow by way of Sweden (where her brother lived).

Kar had purchased a Rolleiflex camera in 1957 that was well suited to the documentary picture stories about London life which, promoted by Kasmin, she began to shoot regularly for the *Tatler & Bystander*. In May 1959 her portfolio of eight commercial gallery owners was published. It included portraits of Picasso's dealer Dudley Tooth, Erica Brausen at the Hanover Gallery (p.96) and Arthur

Bust of Ida Kar by Nikogos Nikogosyan,
1957

Cover of the *Tatler & Bystander*,
8 October 1958

Ida Kar's father, Melkon Karamian,
1957

21

Jeffress against his painted portrait by Graham Sutherland (above). Sutherland's wife Kathleen wrote to Kar, 'How excellent we thought the photographs of art dealers. Especially the Jeffress one (he is thrilled with it I think).'[16] Further photo-essays included 'The West End Arcadians' in the 25 November issue and 'Oriental Religions Among Us' in the 23 December issue, which featured Kar's photographs of Buddhists, Sikhs, Hindus and Muslims living in London. In the summer of 1959 she travelled again to Armenia and Moscow, and a visit to East Germany in September generated several photo-stories of local life. In Dresden she photographed workers at the Hygiene Museum making body-part models and Russian soldiers with paintings they had returned to the Museum of Fine Art after their wartime confiscation. In Stalinstadt she documented a family at home and in East Berlin she visited a home for the elderly. An exhibition of her Armenian photographs was held in Berlin at the palatial Zentrale Haus der Deutsch–Sowjetischen Freundschaft (Central House of German–Soviet Friendship).

However, it was in London that Kar's photographic career had the principal opportunity to thrive. After meeting with Bryan Robertson, director of the

Whitechapel Art Gallery, at one of her homecoming parties, Kar was given the opportunity to exhibit at this prestigious public gallery, where three of her photographs had been seen in spring 1957 as part of a photographic Combined Societies Association travelling exhibition. The Whitechapel was about to host the American abstract expressionist Jackson Pollock's first solo show in Britain (1958), following *This is Tomorrow* (1956), a hugely influential exhibition of young British artists. In July 1958 Robertson wrote to Kar, 'Dear Ida, This is to confirm, subject to the approval of my trustees, that I shall be delighted to organise a large exhibition of your photographic work at this Gallery in 1960.'[17] Robertson supported Kar's ambitions by writing a letter of commendation stating:

> Miss Ida Kar will have a large collective exhibition of her photographic work at this gallery during the course of 1960. Miss Kar is one of the most distinguished and gifted photographers in England, with a first-class European reputation. Her exhibition will be elaborately presented and will undoubtedly be greeted in all quarters as an important event in the artistic and cultural life of London.[18]

A GROUND-BREAKING EXHIBITION

In preparation for her exhibition at the Whitechapel Art Gallery, Kar travelled again to Moscow, this time with her assistant, John Cox. This highly productive visit generated sittings with Leonid Leonov, Nikolai Tomsky (p.32) and Dmitri Shostakovich (p.86). These contributed to a substantial number of Russian portraits exhibited at the Whitechapel.

Taking her commendation letter from Robertson, Kar travelled again to Paris to photograph Eugène Ionesco (p.108), Georges Braque (p.84) and André Breton (p.111). In England she photographed the painter John Bratby (p.101) with his family in Blackheath, Augustus John (p.83) at home in Fordingbridge and Cecil Beaton (p.99), who found the portraits of him taken in Reddish House conservatory to be 'very good indeed'.[19] Kar's technique was described expressively by Jasia Reichardt:

> She talks rapidly while looking around, then starts shooting a single roll of film of twelve shots only, from which the best are selected for printing. The job takes half an hour so that no one has time to get bored. She relies mostly on available natural light and likes strong contrasts. The results: simple, powerful, unaffected, but often dramatic formal revelations of character.[20]

Prior to the opening of her exhibition Kar received financial assistance from a number of supporters. The Whitechapel bore costs for the printing of invitation cards, a catalogue, advertising and publicity, a poster and distribution. Kar's friend Robert Lassam at Kodak assisted with paper supply, but Kar financed the 114 large prints, made by the Autotype Company, with printing costs reaching £800.

Ida Kar: An Exhibition of Artists and Writers in Great Britain, France and the Soviet Union opened at the Whitechapel Art Gallery on 23 March 1960 and during

Ida Kar and a friend at the Whitechapel Art Gallery, 1960

its five-week run received an impressive 10,000 visitors. In his introduction to the catalogue, Colin MacInnes described Kar as

> contribut[ing] a plain feeling for truth, a sympathetic and respectful understanding of the sitter, and a technique which, while [by] no means sensational, is entirely adequate to achieve her ends ... As this exhibition bears effective witness, she is at her most outstanding when photographing fellow artists.[21]

Here MacInnes chanced upon an issue that was to be widely debated by critics, most of whom recognised the artistic achievement of the exhibition. The staging of Kar's work at what had become one of the key venues for significant art exhibitions was an impressive endorsement for photography. Winifred Carr reported in the *Daily Telegraph and Morning Post* that 'Photography ... is being accepted by the rarefied world of serious art ... this is the first time a photographer has actually been invited by an art gallery to give a show.'[22]

Moreover, Kar's large-scale, high-contrast black-and-white prints, which were mounted onto blocked board and for sale as one-offs, bore comparison with paintings. Eric de Maré, writing for the *Observer*, noted that 'The photographs are brilliant and large, some being over four feet wide, revealing beyond further argument that on rare occasions photography can rise to the level of art in its own right.'[23] The unframed photographs were arranged in an irregular but structured formation on the white walls of the gallery (pp.10–11). Kar had been influenced by her visit to Edward Steichen's Museum of Modern Art show, *The Family of Man*, which travelled to London's Royal Festival Hall in 1956, and wrote to Robertson prior to the hanging of her own exhibition:

23

It is two years since I have been planning this exhibition, with John's help, and I have designed the exhibition to suit the gallery; hanging in the way I envisage is 50% of its effectiveness. If it is not hung as we have conceived it we should consider the exhibition ineffective ... Believe me we are going to make this show the most exciting photographic event since *The Family of Man*.[24]

Visitor to Kar's Whitechapel Art Gallery exhibition, by Anthony Panting, 1960

The bold presentation of Kar's work set a precedent for subsequent photographic exhibitions, including a Cecil Beaton retrospective designed by Richard Buckle and held at the National Portrait Gallery in 1968.

The content of Kar's photographs received critical approval. On the BBC programme *The Critics*, David Sylvester said:

> There are several familiar faces which I don't think I shall be able to see again without thinking of Ida Kar's photographs of them. This would be irritating if her vision of these faces were something idiosyncratic interposed between me and the sitters. But Miss Kar does not use her sitters as 'grist for her particular mill'. She has fixed them as they are, accurately and centrally ... To bring out artists and writers, cutting across their view of themselves, is a very remarkable gift indeed.[25]

Kar herself told Rosemary Small at the *Daily Worker*, 'I try to bring out their personality and their background and my own personal interpretation of these things.'[26] Sylvester was adamant, however, that Kar's photographs, despite their brilliance, should not be considered works of art. 'Inasmuch as photography is an art, Ida Kar is an artist, and a very fine one. But I don't think it is an art, because the essence of art is that the artist creates his forms and does not select them: photography reproduces the form.' In a riposte to Sylvester's comment, fellow critic Edgar Anstay thought that Kar's portraits were 'a kind of sophisticated contest of artistic wills'.[27] Beyond the debate over whether her photographs should be considered as works of art, Kar received a positive response in the media, and this, combined with the number of people attending her exhibition, must have led her to believe that she would gain due recognition and that her career would go from strength to strength.

FOLLOWING THE SUCCESS

In April 1961 Gallery One had proved successful enough for Musgrave to move it to new, larger premises in Mayfair, where, according to the *Guardian* critic Eric Newton, it 'emerged in Cinderella-like splendour at 16 North Audley Street, with snow white walls and expensively simple fittings'.[28] Here Kar would photograph the destructivist artist Gustav Metzger at the Fluxus Group's Festival of Misfits, staged at the gallery and the Institute of Contemporary Arts in October 1962, and the painter Bridget Riley at her second solo exhibition (September 1963).

In the spring of 1961, Kar was commissioned by *Queen* magazine to photograph 'Men Who Make Music'. A five-page portfolio included pop impresario

Larry Parnes, music producer and arranger Norrie Paramor and BBC Controller
of Music William Glock. For the *Tatler*, Kar travelled to 'Le Quartier St Ives' in
Cornwall (above). Photographs of Barbara Hepworth through her sculpture *Curved
Form (Trevalgan)*, Peter Lanyon in his garden with his playful daughter Anne-
Marie, Patrick Heron with his family in the grounds of their home Eagles Nest
and Monica Wynter, whose painter husband Bryan was in hospital at the time
of Kar's visit, appeared in the 26 July issue (pp.116–21).

 In April 1962 an exhibition of seventy-six large Whitechapel prints travelled to Moscow's House of Friendship as part of a government-sponsored
cultural exchange programme. Once again, Kar received glowing reviews:
'another victory for one of the most exciting photographic personalities of our
time';[29] 'Ida Kar is that rare thing – the artist photographer';[30] and 'almost
certainly Britain's top art photographer'.[31] The private view was attended by the
wife of First Secretary Nikita Khrushchev, British Ambassador to the Soviet
Union Sir Frank Roberts and Russian photographer Nikolai Svishtov-Paola. The
exhibition was endorsed by Nikolai Tomsky, People's Artist of the USSR, who
wrote of Kar's 'ardent love of art, in whose atmosphere the whole of [her] life is
spent. This love both sharpens and refines the senses.'[32] Twenty thousand
people saw the exhibition in the two weeks it was open and success in the international art press was measured by several pages of coverage in *Motif*, and a
cover story in *Studio*: 'Ida Kar: Artist with a Camera'.[33]

 Kar's commercial portrait work, however, was not so lucrative. She had
been disheartened in 1961, when she was not selected to replace Douglas Glass
as photographer of the *Sunday Times* 'Portrait Gallery'. Consequently, Kar was
pleased to sign a contract with *Animals* magazine in 1963 to photograph in zoos
throughout Britain and Europe. She was often accompanied by eighteen-year-old
Julieta Preston, who had left a photography course at the Regent Street Polytechnic to become Kar's resident assistant (p.27). Photographs taken in Germany

and London for the series 'What is a Zoo?' appeared in issues up to April 1965. Kar's employment of Preston as a pupil in 1961 was the result of a self-confessed disappointment in men. She no longer sought a sexual partnership and, having no children of her own, Preston satisfied Kar's maternal instinct.[34]

In May 1963 *Ida Kar: Artist with a Camera* opened at Birmingham City Museum and Art Gallery. As well as Kar's portraits of artists and writers, the exhibition included a number of her recent animal photographs, some in colour and shown on wall-mounted light boxes. She spoke enthusiastically about her

Self-portrait with a painting by John Christoforou and assemblage by Heinrich Heidersberger, 1962

26

The Chairman and members of the
Museum and Art Gallery Committee
invite you to the private view of the

IDA KAR

ARTIST WITH A CAMERA
EXHIBITION

PHOTOGRAPHS OF ANIMALS
BY COURTESY OF 'ANIMALS' MAGAZINE AND
STUDIES OF FAMOUS ARTISTS AND WRITERS

●

IN THE LECTURE ROOM OF
THE BIRMINGHAM MUSEUM & ART GALLERY
on MONDAY 20th MAY 1963 2.30 p.m. to 6 p.m.

ADMIT TWO

Invitation to the private view at the Birmingham Museum and
Art Gallery, 1963

Julieta Preston (Julie Green), 1963

recent subjects: 'After 25 years of photographing people I found myself getting terribly depressed ... I needed something new ... Like people, animals are full of moods. I hope I shall eventually produce greater creative work in this new field than I have done in portraiture.'[35] Kar may have been reflecting on the increased anxieties in her personal life – her open marriage with Musgrave had become increasingly fraught, and in October 1963 Gallery One closed and Kar and Musgrave moved to 6 Stanhope Place in Bayswater.

The following year provided a new challenge when Kar was invited by the Cuban government to attend the fifth anniversary celebrations of the revolution in Havana in January 1964. She photographed the country's president Fidel Castro at a conference and the poets, artists and writers of a country whose communist ideals she herself embraced. Driven by a government chauffeur, Kar visited Havana, Cojímar and Batabanó. Near Playa Girón, Kar photographed soldiers who had fought in the CIA-sponsored Bay of Pigs invasion. 'We are really witnessing the birth of a nation in Cuba,' she reflected, 'everyone studying, everyone working so hard. The artists are as dynamic as anyone else today in Cuba. I think Fidel Castro's speeches act on people like a tonic, which is not eclipsed even by the heat.'[36]

Portraits of the poet Nicolás Guillén Batista, the artist René Portocarrero, Castro's photographer Alberto Korda and the architect Ricardo Hidalgo on site at the National Art School Havana, were shown alongside a print of a palm-lined road entitled *Dawn over Cuba* and street scenes taken in 'Old Havana' at Mayfair's Hamiltons Gallery and Stepney Central Library in February 1965. Peggy Delius, in the long-established and respected weekly *British Journal of Photography*, described the photographs as 'fresh and strong, without preconceived ideas but in sympathy with her chosen subject.'[37] Kar's Cuban photographs marked the last publicly recognised creative phase of her career, and a move towards a documentary style in accordance with the changing fashions in photography. Delius commented that Kar 'brings to her present exhibition

something new – a documentary quality tinged with a mixture cool, remote, yet full of burning observation. Clearly the emergence of the new Cuba has touched her creative ability profoundly.'[38]

In 1968, following Preston's departure, John Couzins became one of Kar's last assistants (and was to remain with her until 1971). A photograph of Kar with Couzins and three other students at Rex Place, where she lived with Musgrave until 1969, is suggestive of Kar's continued desire for companionship (p.30). Couzins assisted Kar on her shoot with Bill Brandt in 1968. The resulting portraits (p.138) demonstrate Kar's continuing ability in the year in which she exhibited at the Midland Arts Centre, alongside Brandt and Bill Jay as well as Preston and Couzins.

Throughout the late 1960s, Kar's behaviour became increasingly erratic and she suffered from severe depression, spending a number of periods as a patient in St Mary Abbots psychiatric hospital in London. For a period in 1968 she lived in Paris, with the aim of making reportage photographs. She stayed in seven hotels there, financially assisted by the Salvation Army, with whom she sang on a Sunday. While living in the city Kar became unwell and was moved to St Anne's psychiatric hospital, where she photographed the building and staff, but wrote in protest about the way she, 'an artist', had been treated.[39]

Kar and Musgrave had previously spent periods living apart and in 1969 Musgrave, remembered as having a calm and intellectual demeanour, began a separation from Kar which would last the rest of her lifetime. Around this time Kar often visited St Sarkis, the Armenian Orthodox Church in Kensington, and her Armenian heritage became increasingly important in her later years. Despite her failing health and periods of hospitalisation, Kar remained committed to her work and in the summer of 1974 embarked on a project photographing nudes. She photographed a man, a pregnant woman and a young couple posing in a make-shift studio in her bedsit at 47 Inverness Terrace, Bayswater. The contact sheets show that the portrait of her father (p.20), included in her Whitechapel exhibition, had been removed from its hook for the duration of the session. Clearly intending these photographs for public use, Kar ordered enlargements of the retouched images. She was recording her autobiography onto tapes (now lost) when she died alone of a cerebral haemorrhage on 24 December 1974.

IDA KAR'S PLACE IN PHOTOGRAPHIC HISTORY

In Kar's lifetime several of her portraits were collected by national galleries. In 1966 the Victoria and Albert Museum wrote to Kar asking for sixteen of her favourite portraits for touring exhibitions; these included portraits of Georges Braque, Jacob Epstein and Barbara Hepworth. In the same year the influential photo-historian Helmut Gernsheim, one of Kar's key champions, arranged for his collection housed at the University of Texas to acquire 124 of Kar's exhibition prints. He included her in his 1962 survey *Creative Photography: Aesthetic Trends 1839–1960*, writing that Kar's 'reportage style of portraiture conveys the personality of the sitter through the atmosphere of his own surroundings'[40] and in the introduction to her 1963 Birmingham exhibition catalogue Gernsheim noted that the most remarkable feature of Kar's work was 'the feeling of depth and spaciousness.'[41]

It was not until December 1982 that sixty of Kar's works were assembled by John Kasmin, who held an exhibition of *Vintage Photographs by Ida Kar* at the Knoedler Kasmin Gallery, Cork Street, London. In the accompanying brochure Victor Musgrave wrote: 'It hurts to write about Ida. Omnivorous and vulnerable both, her voice and eyes allied with the extraordinary things she said could win people's hearts or provoke them to fury. Few remained indifferent to her, nor would she have wished them to.'[42] A *Time Out* critic asked 'Why isn't this woman world-famous for her sympathetic but keen eye?'[43] Prints sold included six portraits of artists to gallery owner Leslie Waddington and a print of Craigie Aitchison bought by Jasper Conran. When the exhibition travelled to the Scottish Gallery in Edinburgh, director Bill Jackson noted that 'it proved to be an immensely popular exhibition and many people preferred it to the Brandt and McBean exhibitions which were in Edinburgh at the same time.'[44]

Seeking to raise Ida Kar's profile, Val Williams wrote a thoroughly researched monograph, *Ida Kar: Photographer 1908–1974*, which was published by Virago Press in 1989. Monika Kinley, the subsequent partner of Victor Musgrave, was the steward of the archive and granted Williams free access. A co-ordinated exhibition held at London's Zelda Cheatle Gallery in October of the same year received positive reviews.

In 1981 the National Portrait Gallery purchased twenty vintage prints of Kar's most established sitters through Dorothy Bohm of the Photographers' Gallery on behalf of Victor Musgrave. However, a more significant acquisition occurred in 1999, when the National Portrait Gallery purchased the complete surviving Ida Kar archive, which comprises eight hundred photographic prints, ten thousand negatives, four hundred vintage contact prints, exhibition catalogues, correspondence, press cuttings and the ownership of Kar's copyright.

The subconscious arrangements of bottles, books and brushes in Kar's portraits inform the viewer of the working methods and lifestyles of major writers and artists. The surviving negatives tell a more comprehensive story. Kar's oeuvre is remarkable both for its aesthetic accomplishment and as a social commentary on cultural life in mid-twentieth-century Europe. With this exhibition and publication the National Portrait Gallery continues its tradition of reappraising women photographers and presents the significant output of a complex and committed artist.[45]

Ida Kar with her assistants, including John Couzins, by John Couzins, 1968

1 *Evening Standard*, 23 March 1960.
2 Reichardt, Jasia, *Art News and Review*, 26 March–9 April 1960.
3 Harrison, Martin, *Transition: The London Art Scene in the Fifties* (London: Merrell, 2002).
4 'London Art Tripping', interview with Bill Hopkins by Stewart Home, 2006.
5 Robins, Brian, 'The Farm', unpublished MS. Collection John Cox.
6 Camera Press sales reports, dated 1981–2 and 1983–4. Ida Kar archive, National Portrait Gallery.
7 Butler, Reg, letter to Ida Kar, 8 September 1954. Ida Kar archive, National Portrait Gallery.
8 Hopkins, Bill, 'French Painters of Today', unpublished typescript, 1954. Ida Kar archive, National Portrait Gallery.
9 *Art News and Review*, October 1954.
10 Kar, Ida, letter to John Kasmin, 14 September 1958. Ida Kar archive, National Portrait Gallery.
11 *Vogue*, March 1956.
12 Gould, Tony, *Inside Outsider: The Life and Times of Colin MacInnes* (London: Chatto & Windus, 1983), p.110.
13 MacInnes, Colin, quoted in ibid., p.110.
14 Taylor, Terry, unpublished interview with the author, February 2009.
15 Ibid.
16 Sutherland, Mrs G., letter to Ida Kar, 28 May 1959. Ida Kar archive, National Portrait Gallery.
17 Robertson, Bryan, letter to Ida Kar, 11 July 1958. Whitechapel Gallery archive.
18 Robertson, Bryan, letter 'to whom it may concern', 11 May 1959. Ida Kar archive, National Portrait Gallery.
19 Beaton, Cecil, letter to Ida Kar, undated. Ida Kar archive, National Portrait Gallery.
20 Reichardt, Jasia, *Art News and Review*, 26 March–9 April 1960.
21 Whitechapel Art Gallery exhibition catalogue, 1960.
22 Carr, Winifred, *Daily Telegraph and Morning Post*, 4 March 1960.
23 Mare, Eric de, *Observer*, 27 March 1960.
24 Kar, Ida, letter to Bryan Robertson, 1959. Ida Kar archive, National Portrait Gallery. The 'John' referred to is Kar's assistant John Cox, who is thanked in the catalogue acknowledgements.
25 BBC programme, *The Critics*, 24 April 1960. Transcript in press cuttings book, Ida Kar archive, National Portrait Gallery.
26 Small, Rosemary, *Daily Worker*, n.d.
27 BBC programme, *The Critics*, 24 April 1960. Transcript in press cuttings book, Ida Kar archive, National Portrait Gallery.
28 Newton, Eric, 'The London Galleries', *Guardian*, 25 May 1961.
29 *British Journal of Photography*, March 1962.
30 *Tatler*, 21 March 1962.
31 *Harper's Bazaar*, March 1962.
32 Tomsky, Nikolai, 'The Art of Ida Kar', 1962. Letter in press cuttings book, Ida Kar archive, National Portrait Gallery.
33 'Ida Kar: Artist with a Camera', *Studio*, February 1962.
34 Green, Julie, unpublished interview with the author, February 2009.
35 *Evening Mail and Despatch*, 20 May 1963.
36 Kar, Ida, 'Impressions of my visit to Cuba', unpublished MS, 1964. Ida Kar archive, National Portrait Gallery.
37 Delius, Peggy, *British Journal of Photography*, 12 February 1965.
38 Ibid.
39 Kar, Ida, unpublished MS, *c*.1968–9. Collection John Couzins.
40 Gernsheim, Helmut, *Creative Photography: Aesthetic Trends 1839–1960* (London: Faber & Faber, 1962).
41 Gernsheim, Helmut, 'The Photographs of Ida Kar', leaflet to accompany Birmingham Art Gallery exhibition, 1963.
42 Kasmin Knoedler Gallery exhibition brochure.
43 *Time Out*, 14–20 January 1983.
44 Jackson, William C.M., letter to Ms Antoinette Godkin, 15 April 1983. Ida Kar archive, National Portrait Gallery.
45 Previous exhibitions have presented Madame Yevonde (*Colour, Fantasy & Myth*, 1990), Dorothy Wilding (*The Pursuit of Perfection*, 1991), Rollie McKenna (*Artists and Writers*, 2001) and Lee Miller (*Portraits*, 2005).

Nikolai Tomsky, 1959

BEYOND THE MERE LIKENESS
KAREN WRIGHT

AS A WRITER and editor I am aware of the appeal of photographs and texts that relate to artists at work in the studio. Access to the working world of an artist helps shed valuable light onto the production of their works. In this time of increasing celebrity appeal it also provides a little glamour in the eye of the viewer; that additional information which can excite interest in the work. Alongside other post-war photographers – such as Henri Cartier-Bresson, who recorded Alberto Giacometti's artistic practice for many years; Hans Namuth, whose famous images of Jackson Pollock at work continue to be reproduced; Ugo Mulas, who documented both Italian and American artists; and David Douglas Duncan, whose photographs of Picasso were published in a series of books from 1958 – Ida Kar helped to open the door for public interest in the intimacy of the artist's studio.

Going into an artist's studio is an intrusion into an intimate space, and it takes sensitivity to be able to establish a relationship with the artist. Kar became familiar with the contemporary art scene in London through her marriage to the writer and gallery-owner Victor Musgrave, as their home was a meeting point for artists and writers. She met and developed relationships with several artists, including Ivon Hitchens and Josef Herman, whom she was later to photograph, as well as writers such as Colin MacInnes, who would become a lodger in their house. Kar established and sustained a close relationship with John Kasmin, who worked for her in the 1950s before starting his own gallery. He vividly recalls that she was 'always in an art environment, as Soho was then full of artists, writers and theatrical people using the bars, cafes and clubs to meet, talk, use whores, gamble, gambol, drink and drugs. A real pool of talent and easy meetings.'[1] Kar enjoyed her proximity to this scene, and this is reflected in many of her photographs, which capture the intimacy between people and place.

Recording the relationship between the artist and their work was something Kar relished. In a portrait of Ivon Hitchens at home in Sussex in 1954 (p.64), Kar integrates into her composition the details of an artist's studio, the bottles of solvents and dirty rags, as well as giving the viewer a hint of Hitchens's work, posing him seemingly relaxed in front of his easel, on which we can see vigorous charcoal drawings. Similarly, in a portrait of Henry Moore taken at his studio (p.63), his sculptures appear like living entities, and the silhouetted figure in the foreground seems to appear as a ghostly presence of what Moore is considering. Another portrait, of the Russian sculptor Nikolai Tomsky looking up at his large

André Breton with his wife, Elisa, 1960

sculpture of Lenin (p.32), achieves startling psychological insight. There is a Pygmalion quality here, as the artist has created a work of art that far outstrips his own power. Tomsky's expression is particularly disquieting, as if the artist knows he has let an evil genie out of the bottle.

While many of Kar's portraits of artists were taken in studios or in galleries, some were made in the sitters' homes. The Japanese artist Tsugouharu Foujita, for example, is portrayed surrounded by three porcelain dolls (p.78). If Foujita chose this location, it seems an appropriate one. Many of his painted images seem somewhat removed from reality.

In images that depict more than one person, Kar often comments on the relationships she perceives between her sitters. One portrait of André Breton includes his wife, Elisa, with the couple seen in their apartment surrounded by their intriguing collection of objets d'art (above). Kar shows Breton slightly in the foreground, with Elisa sitting behind, and captures the almost furtive glance that Elisa is directing at her husband, shedding light on Kar's perception of their relationship. It is clear here that Elisa is in a supporting role to the more dominant Breton. Beautifully lit, this photograph displays Kar's talent for engaging with her sitters' environment.

Tenderness is not something that one automatically associates with Kar's work, but it is clearly demonstrated in her portrait of Bryan Wynter's wife, Monica, and their young son (opposite), included in her 1961 portfolio of St Ives artists shot for the *Tatler*. The painter Bryan Wynter was sick in hospital at the time, so his wife substituted for the artist in the studio shoot. Whether it was worry about her husband or merely the skill of the photographer, Wynter seems totally oblivious to the photographer. Her maternal gaze is directed solely at her child. However, it is not really Wynter's family that are the stars of the image, but the studio. The presence of the artist is replaced by his canvases, both in progress and waiting to be worked on. The table top, with the large pot of well-used brushes, is illuminated by the painterly light suffusing the room.

In another, slightly earlier, portrait, the kitchen-sink artist John Bratby ostensibly admonishes his young son while his wife and fellow artist, Jean Cooke, looks on, seemingly approvingly (p.101). Kar has carefully composed the family in front of their home. There is no sense of depth to the space, as there is in many of Kar's images. It is as if the family are in a picture frame themselves, formed by the horizontal porch structure on which Cooke is seated, the only depth suggested by the windows of the Bratby portrait behind Cooke. There is no presentiment here of the tension between Cooke and Bratby that would lead eventually to their divorce.

It seems that working with more than one sitter enabled Kar to capture something intangible – the relationship between the two sitters, or, in the case of an arresting portrait of philosopher Bertrand Russell sitting for Sir Jacob Epstein, a triangular relationship (p.143). Here the artist is shown totally engaged with the image of his sitter, while Russell seems relaxed, albeit holding a difficult pose with his hand up holding his pipe. Kar manages somehow in this set-up to show the somewhat bemused expression of Russell as he is captured for posterity, while the artist appears more involved with the inanimate object than the real sitter in front of him.

Monica Wynter and her son, 1961

Josef Herman, 1960

Jackson Pollock, by Hans Namuth, 1950

Kar was conscious of the need to create a space for her subjects, and captured them in close-up relatively infrequently. Among her photographs is a portrait of the artist Josef Herman (opposite), a friend of Kar's who had been a frequent visitor to her home and who had enjoyed her famously good cooking. At her death he said that she 'left a vacuum that no-one else could fill. She was a complete original.'[2] Kar's photograph of Herman at work in his studio evokes the intimacy of the workplace for the viewer. She chooses to include clues about Herman's identity as an artist – the kettle on the far right speaks of the artist's time spent alone and at work. Herman's religiousness (he was a practising Jew) is here represented by the menorah candlestick on the fireplace, while his interest in primitive art (of which he had amassed an impressive collection) is evident in the works hung on the wall. Kar chooses to photograph him from above, distancing herself from the subject. He is apparently unaware of her presence, engaged in mixing colours on the flat palette for the large painting propped on the easel.

Kar's approach to portraiture contrasts with that taken by her contemporaries. Her study of Herman is an action shot, but a gentle one, with none of the high drama or energy of, for example, the more famous photographs by Hans Namuth of Jackson Pollock at work (above). When Namuth's photographs were first published in *Portfolio* in 1951, they quickly came to familiarise the world with the face of the artist but also helped to validate his practice, opening the door to the naming of the school as 'action painters'. It allowed the public access to the artist's method and helped explain not only how the works were made – horizontally on the floor, the artist spattering paint from a large can of domestic paint – but also the dynamic physicality of the process. It was these images – heroic, romantic – that helped to increase public interest in the artist and his studio.

Lucio Fontana, by Ugo Mulas, 1964

In his portrait of Lucio Fontana, Ugo Mulas seemingly captures the moment when Fontana was about to cut into his canvas (left). Mulas was a friend of the artist in Milan and would often drive over to see him, without a tripod or lights, to shoot what he was doing. Mulas later confessed that this photograph was not taken as the artist worked but was instead a set-up shot. Fontana had refused to be photographed working, justifying this by telling Mulas that it was not the cut that was important but the thinking before he took the action with his Stanley knife; in Mulas' words, 'how the preparatory moment, the one before the cut, was the most important, the decisive one'.[3] Knowing that it was a set-up shot does not lessen the portrait's impact, and, like the image by Kar of Epstein and Russell, the seeming obliviousness of subject to photographer leads to an understanding of the process of making art.

Kar's strong sense of the artist in context, seen for example in the Herman portrait, differs from the style adopted by other contemporaries. Jane Bown, for example, chose to show the emerging artist David Hockney not in his studio or in front of a work, but instead in close-up (below). Hockney is seen unflinching before the camera, his eyes visible through thick, black-rimmed glasses. He looks both vulnerable and cocky. What is clear is the spirit of investigation that Bown has palpably captured. Similarly, John Deakin's photograph of the late sculptor Eduardo Paolozzi as a young man shows the sitter in close-up, capturing the toughness of the artist (opposite, top). His pugilistic quality can be seen in his mouth, and even his hair, springy and unruly, almost crisp-looking, is full of energy, although antithetically, the artist's head, resting on his hand, is calm.

Deakin was among the first British photographers to have a personal relationship with artists that led to him photographing several of his subjects. Among his sitters was the writer Colin MacInnes, who was also Kar's lodger and a favourite subject of hers. One of Deakin's images of MacInnes shows the writer beautifully lit but somehow rendered anonymous by the empty space around him. Kar's series of images, by contrast, illustrate an even closer relationship between photographer and sitter. Even when MacInnes is stretched out on the bed reading, it is clear in the shape of his body that he is fully engaged with the photographer (p.103). There is an evident intimacy between the photographer and the photographed, seen in MacInnes' relaxed pose, and a use of the

David Hockney,
by Jane Bown, 1966

Eduardo Paolozzi, by John Deakin, 1952

space for dramatic effect, something that we also see in, for example, one of Kar's portraits of Iris Murdoch (below). This image shows a writer kneeling by her bed in front of a scattered manuscript, as if about to pounce, again totally engaged with the photographer, almost provoking the camera's gaze. This portrait, like her various portraits of MacInnes, show an unusual depth of engagement by Kar, and lead the viewer to understand the isolation of creative people, who lead a primarily isolated and solitary life.

Some of Kar's most interesting portraits, including those of Murdoch, are of women. In her photographs of Bridget Riley (overleaf and p.133), whom she captures as a young woman in 1963 posing at an exhibition of her work, Kar elects to depict the artist in front of her easily identifiable swirling black-and-white artworks. What could have been an uninteresting image comes to life through the dramatic, almost defiant, angle of the artist's profile. In 1961 Kar photographed the St Ives-based artist Barbara Hepworth for the *Tatler* (pp.41, 117). Hepworth was notoriously tough, not surprisingly, as she chose sculpture – a medium dominated by men. An image of Hepworth in her studio is one of my favourites among Kar's portraits. Rather than showing the domesticity of the studio – the kettle in the Josef Herman image – or the austerity of the Riley portrait, Kar chooses to portray Hepworth seemingly at work snipping wires for an armature. The lattice of the wire veils the square and no-nonsense face of the artist, who, while dressed in working clothes, is wearing a highly decorative necklace. Whether or not Kar is consciously alluding to the metaphor of the

39

Iris Murdoch, 1957

cage, it is certainly implied that being a sculptor was not, at this time, an easy career for a woman, portrayed here almost literally imprisoned by her gender, caught in the expectations of a medium still largely practised by men. While the cage may appear to be a harsh critique of chauvinism, it also softens the subject's blunt features, making Hepworth beautiful.

As a strong-minded woman making a career in a male-dominated art form, Kar would have understood the challenges facing Hepworth. Kar encountered an additional difficulty, for although by the 1960s photography had become increasingly acceptable as an artistic medium, it was caught in the perpetual argument as to its purpose: subject-led documentation or art form? This debate was central to contemporary critical reception of Kar's work. Indeed it remains a point of discussion today as people continue to look at photographs for different reasons. For some, they are records of a time and place, and one looks hoping to learn more about the subject, through clues in their surroundings, posture or expression. For others, it is much more of an aesthetic experience, admiring the photographer's technique, examining the tonality and enjoying the 'eye-filling-ness' of the work. Yet what is exciting about Kar's oeuvre is that it spans these possibilities. In the group of works she shot in Cuba in 1964, Kar moved between portraits of the country's leading creative and political figures and more anonymous subject matter. In both types of photograph she shows her skill in selecting what may appear to be casual choices, but are instead powerful images. Here

Bridget Riley, 1963

Barbara Hepworth, 1961

is a woman, standing at the open window of a roadside drinks stand, whom Kar chooses to shoot from the rear (below). She is wearing a tight, flowered dress that emphasises her curvy figure. The photograph contrasts the energy inherent in the woman with the pin-up girl painted on the outer wall, who is blank-faced and drained of life in comparison. It records, too, poverty in the patched and damaged roof.

At the bar in Cojímar, 1964

John Latham and John Kasmin, 1963

42

The casual, caught moment was not only used in Kar's anonymous works. Two of her portraits, of Gustav Metzger (p.134) and of John Latham (p.135), show an element of serendipity as well. Metzger is captured posed in front of the window of her husband's gallery, the logo seen at the top. It looks as if it could have been taken in his studio with the scribbled words, maybe on the window itself, and with the ambiguous positioning of the chair, it seems to be almost an office environment, far from the more familiar white cube. In the contact sheets of Kar's portraits taken in John Latham's studio, Kasmin appears in some of the frames. Kasmin recalls that 'Latham was a great friend and under contract to me for a few years from 1961 to 1964.'[4] My favourite is a shot in which Kasmin is crouched next to the conceptual artist Latham, obviously relating something to the artist who appears to be more engaged with his inner thoughts than with his dealer's conversation (above).

Like all of Kar's best photographs, whether they were conceived as documentary works to record her encounters with leading cultural figures or artistic responses to the places she visited, this image manages to capture something beyond the 'mere' likeness. Consider the group of photographs documenting the arcades of central London, which Kar took in 1959 on commission for the *Tatler*. In one, a man in a clothes shop lurks discreetly in the shadows, while in the foreground, the gleaming white of a glove on a stand speaks for his pride in his profession. In contrast, in another image taken in the Burlington Arcade, Clive

**Clive Allen with a customer
(The Burlington Arcade),** 1959

Allen, owner of the Roods jewellery shop, shows his client some of his wares (above). Kar here, as in some of her other portraits containing couples, manages to capture a moment between the two, the woman focused not as one would naturally expect on the shiny jewels but on the man serving her. He has the gravitas and stature of the owner of the establishment, and there is an engagement between the seller and the buyer that sparks the imagination. These images provide a snapshot of a moment in time and are beautifully nuanced, full of space and tonality – every gradient of white, grey and black is represented here, Kar's use of light giving us insights into the desires and aspirations of her subjects.

More than half a century after Kar's milestone exhibition at the Whitechapel Art Gallery in 1960, the argument continues as to whether photography is as important a medium as painting, sculpture, installation and conceptual art. Major contemporary practitioners still strive to avoid being compartmentalised by the label 'photographer'. Kar broke new ground by declaring herself to be an 'artist with a camera' in the title of her 1963 Birmingham exhibition; someone who resisted pure documentation, moving beyond the mere likeness. She managed, in her portraits of artists and writers and in her finely observed artistic images, to provide insights into both her own artistry and the creativity of her subjects. In a powerful image, a nude portrait with child, taken after her marriage with Musgrave had broken down and when she was alone and living in a bedsit, Kar portrays a mother and child (p.139). They are both nude and the child is not young. The mother, unlike Monica Wynter, is not engaged with the child, but stares forward into space, while the child cups her mother's breast. It is a strong image, disproving any notion that the photographer's powers tailed off in later life, and reinforcing Kar's ability to capture an emotion through the lens.

1   Kasmin, John, in an email to the author, 5 September 2010.
2   Williams, Val, *Ida Kar: Photographer 1908–1974* (London: Virago Press, 1989), p.70.
3   Ugo Mulas website (www.ugomulas.org).
4   Kasmin, John, in an email to the author, 9 October 2010.

FROM THE ARCHIVE

The value of Ida Kar's own work as a photographer is self-evident as a record for us and for the future, but her intelligence and integrity are behind every picture and so her photographs go further than records: we look at these faces and are engrossed by them because each face seems to be formed by that effort to project a particular life and experience into a particular kind of work which we find reflected in artists' faces. We feel, in fact, some slight sensation of what it is to be an artist. And the range of human expression is so wide in her photographs that they make us look with a fresh awareness at faces around us, in life.

Bryan Robertson; from the preface to the catalogue of Kar's exhibition at the Whitechapel Art Gallery, 1960

This gift – to woo and win intimacy without any loss of courteous defence – is one Ida Kar possesses because of her own gift for life and unaffected love of it, which will explain, as much as any photographic talent, the immediate charm and psychological simplicity of the images she makes. Her subjects stand revealed: but never mockingly 'exposed' or 'glamourised' with patronage, or loaded by any egotistical obsessions of the photographer. She tells us what kind of man it is who's posed for her, a great deal about the quality of his own work and, indirectly, quite a lot about herself.

Colin MacInnes; from the introduction to the catalogue of Kar's exhibition at the Whitechapel Art Gallery, 1960

This is photography at its best and portraiture at its most human.
Guardian, **26 March 1960**

The photographs [in Kar's Whitechapel Gallery exhibition] are brilliant and large, some being over four feet wide, revealing beyond further argument that on rare occasions photography can rise to the level of an art in its own right. They also show that personal vision is much more important than obsessive mechanical skill in making that immediate visual impact which marks a good photograph – especially in portraiture where aesthetic success depends far less on technique and costly equipment than on visual sensibility, instinctive choice of the significant split-second at which to press the trigger and that rapport which the photographer must establish with his subject.

Eric de Maré, 'Art from a Camera', *Observer*, 27 March 1960

Epstein sculpting Bertrand Russell—1953.

PHOTOGRAPHS AS WORKS OF ART

CELEBRATED SITTERS

Men and women celebrated in the arts come vividly before the eye in the remarkable series of photographs by Ida Karr, on view from to-day and during April at the Whitechapel Art Gallery. The personality of the sitters—writers, painters, sculptors and others—is sympathetically and often dramatically interpreted in terms of light and shade; of Marc Chagall, with a bird-like gesture of the hand; of Somerset Maugham, deeply reflective; of Epstein and Bertrand Russell in an evidently happy relation of sculptor and model; of Augustus John in great dignity.

The photographs may be considered as works of art in themselves, for the effect is often gained by some carefully considered and unusually distinguished treatment of space or placing which has a value of its own: such as that which poses Sir John Rothenstein so impressively in the largeness of the sculpture gallery at the Tate or adds its interest of design to the portrait of Mr. Dudley Tooth. The large scale of most of the exhibited prints brings the design factor into prominence. The visual arts come off best, perhaps, for here the photographer is able to set sitter and work together. There are glimpses of studios, such as that of Barqué, and the work of art is frequently interpreted or presented with no less sympathy than its creator. Very happy, for instance, is the use of one of L. S. Lowry's industrial city scenes as a background for the painter in person.

45

From *The Times,* 1960

The wonderful portraits Julia Margaret Cameron produced of the Great Victorians in the 1860s were prophesied by Roger Fry 'to outlive most of the works of the artists who were her contemporaries'. We marvel at her depth of understanding, her characterization, which gave us such compelling likenesses. The same can be said of Ida Kar's portrait studies, although she no longer favours the close-up, which brings the onlooker into close contact with the sitter. That intimacy which J.M. Cameron established between us and her sitters by bringing them physically close to us, Ida Kar conveys in a different way, by depicting the sitter in his own surroundings, the atmosphere created by his personality.
Helmut Gernsheim; from the brochure accompanying Kar's exhibition at the Birmingham Art Gallery, 1963

For many years, as her reputation began to grow, I had the experience of seeing many of the world's famous faces climb the stairs of our house to the top floor, where they would find her awaiting them in our bedroom, which was where she usually preferred to photograph them. And at times she would invade their homes. Either way it could be a disconcerting experience as Ida tried to possess the soul of the sitter through the lens of her primitive camera.
Victor Musgrave; from the leaflet accompanying the exhibition of Kar's work at the Kasmin Knoedler Gallery, 1982

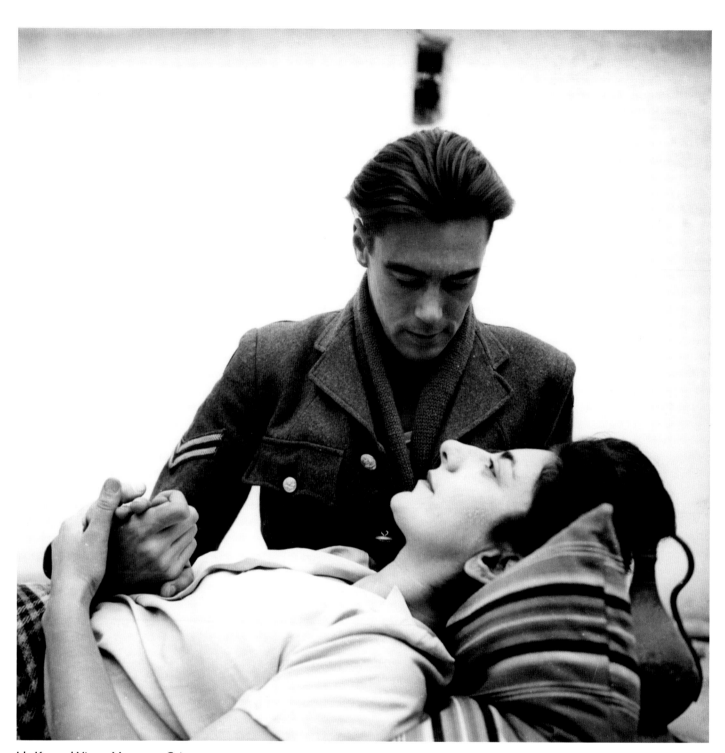

Ida Kar and Victor Musgrave, Cairo, 1944

CHRONOLOGY

1908 Ida Karamian was born on 8 April in Tambov, Russia, to Armenian parents. Her father, Melkon, was a teacher of mathematics, physics, French and Persian. Ida spent her childhood in Armenia, Russia and Iran.

1921 The Karamian family moved to Alexandria, Egypt, where Melkon pursued his teaching career. Ida, the only daughter, was educated at the prestigious Lycée Français in Alexandria.

1928–9 Kar continued her education in Paris, where, with her father's encouragement, she began studying medicine and chemistry before pursuing singing and the violin. Through these music studies she became acquainted with the pianist (and future wife of the playwright Samuel Beckett) Suzanne Dechevaux-Dumesnil (1900–89), who introduced Kar to the German surrealist painter and photographer Heinrich Heidersberger (1906–2006). With Heidersberger Kar produced her first experimental photographs, and through him she came to know many writers and artists living on the Left Bank.

1933 Kar returned to Egypt and lived with her parents in the Rue Tanis, Alexandria, where she found life restrictive after her years in cosmopolitan Paris. Problems with her voice led Kar to abandon her plans for a singing career.

1935 After a chance meeting with a Hungarian photographer, Kar started work as his assistant and receptionist. She was able to use the photographer's facilities, and made a number of portraits of her friends and relations.

Late 1930s Kar married Edmond Belali, an Egyptian government official who was also a keen amateur photographer. They moved to Cairo and established the photographic studio 'Idabel' in a fashionable part of the city.

1937 Kar's parents returned to live in Yerevan (Erevan), Armenia.

1942 Victor Musgrave (1919–84), writer, artist and advocate of the avant-garde, was drafted to Cairo as an non-commissioned officer in the Royal Air Force. He published and edited *Contact*, the first services periodical to appear in the Middle East, and wrote art criticism for the *Egyptian Gazette*.

Ida Kar and a friend, early 1920s

Ida Kar's parents, early 1940s

Self-portrait, Alexandria, 1933

Ida Kar and Victor Musgrave outside the Mercury Theatre, Cairo, 1944

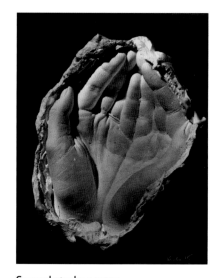

Surreal study, *c.*1947

48

Ida Kar and Theodore Garman, early 1950s

1943–4 The Idabel studio exhibited in two surrealist *Art and Freedom* group exhibitions staged in Cairo.

1944 Following a divorce from Belali, Kar married Victor Musgrave. After a honeymoon in Palestine, they set up home in the Darb el-Labana district of Cairo, where they entertained many international artists and writers.

1945 Kar and Musgrave left Egypt after the end of the war and moved into a small flat at 34b Devonshire Close, London W1, near Regent's Park. The austerity of post-war Britain was a great contrast to their lifestyle in Egypt.

1946 Kar arranged with Olwen Vaughan, former secretary of the British Film Institute, to show some of her work at the New London Film Society.

1947 Kar exhibited alongside the sculptor Robert Couturier at the Anglo-French Art Centre in St John's Wood, north London. She advertised for commissions as a 'theatrical photographer', and some of the resulting portraits appeared in the stage and screen casting directory *Spotlight*. Kar rented a darkroom from the literary photographer Mark Gerson, a lifelong friend.

1949 Kar and Musgrave moved to 1 Litchfield Street, just off Charing Cross Road, where the painter John Christoforou had opened a small gallery. Musgrave was appointed by Christoforou to staff the gallery, and Kar established a small studio on an upper floor.

1951–4 Kar assisted in the guardianship of Theodore Garman (1924–54), an artist suffering from mental illness who was the only son of Jacob Epstein and Kathleen Garman. During this time Kar had access to Epstein's studio and took photographs at a number of sculpture sittings, including those with Somerset Maugham (published in the *Observer*, 11 November 1951) and Bertrand Russell, which was the first of Kar's photographs to be syndicated by Camera Press.

Kar travelled to Italy with Theodore Garman. While there she photographed the art dealer Peggy Guggenheim with her lover Raoul Gregorich at the Palazzo Venier dei Leoni on Venice's Grand Canal (Guggenheim's house and collection had opened to the public annually in the summer months from 1951).

1952 Kar attended *Photographs by Henri Cartier-Bresson* at the Institute of Contemporary Arts (ICA), the first showing of his work in London. She continued to photograph actors and actresses with strong lighting and tight cropping. Portraits of this kind include those of Tutte Lemkow (p.58), then appearing on screen in *Moulin Rouge*, and his actress wife Mai Zetterling, photographed the following year. Kar photographed Stephen Spender both formally and at home with his children, Matthew and Lizzie, the first of three sittings with the poet.

1953 Christoforou moved from London to work in Paris and Provence. Musgrave took over the running of the Litchfield Street gallery. Kar began a series of photographs of artists and writers. In December Musgrave opened Gallery One at 1 Litchfield Street with a group show of paintings by John Christoforou, sculpture by Peter Danziger and gouaches and etchings by Sam Kramer.

1954 Kar travelled to Paris to photograph artists in their studios. Her sitters included Camille Bombois (p.79), Massimo Campigli with Susanne Rodillon, Marc Chagall (p.71), Le Corbusier (below), Tsuguoharu Foujita (p.78), Alberto Giacometti (p.77), Marcel Gromaire, Marie Laurencin (p.73), Fernand Léger (p.70), Joan Miró, Man Ray (p.72), Germaine Richier (p.76), Gino Severini (p.75), Pierre Soulages, Jacques Villon and Ossip Zadkine (p.87).

On her return to England, Kar continued to photograph British artists in preparation for her Gallery One exhibition; sitters this year included Kenneth Armitage (p.66), Reg Butler (p.67), Lynn Chadwick, John Christoforou, Jacob Epstein (p.60), William Gear. Ivon Hitchens (p.64), L.S. Lowry, Henry Moore (p.63), Victor Pasmore, William Scott, Feliks Topolski (p.82), Stanley Spencer (p.65), John Piper (p.68) and Graham Sutherland (p.69).

Kar's exhibition *Forty Artists from London and Paris* ran at Gallery One from 12 to 31 October 1954.

Bill Hopkins, a writer, moved in with Kar and Musgrave as a lodger.

Peggy Guggenheim, *c.*1953

Stephen Spender with his children Lizzie and Matthew, 1952

Le Corbusier, page from Kar's Artists album, Paris, 1954

Elisabeth Frink, 1956

Ida Kar arriving in Moscow, by Galina Sanko, 1958

Patrick Magee in *Krapp's Last Tape***,** 1958

1955 Kar began to photograph artists showing at Gallery One, such as F.N. Souza who had his first exhibition at the Gallery in February. Gallery One closed in September, and Musgrave and Kar moved to a larger building at 20 D'Arblay Street in Soho. Kar's portrait of Henry Moore was published in the November issue of *Vogue*.

Kar was painted by Josef Herman. The title of the portrait, *A Friend*, reflected their companionship, which lasted a number of years. Kar photographed Herman in the mid-1950s and in 1960, as well taking reference photographs of his artworks.

1956 In March Gallery One re-opened in the D'Arblay Street premises with an exhibition of watercolours by Henry Miller. John Kasmin (who later became a gallery owner and art dealer) began to work for Musgrave in the gallery and for Kar, promoting her work and organising sittings, including the first of two sittings with poet T.S. Eliot and the young sculptor Elisabeth Frink. The writer Colin MacInnes became a lodger at D'Arblay Street and a friend of Kar, as well as an admirer of her work.

1957 In the spring three of Kar's photographs were shown in the upper rooms of the Whitechapel Art Gallery as part of a travelling exhibition organised by the Combined Societies Association. Subsequently Kar was commissioned to return to Armenia (then a Soviet republic) for the first time since her childhood. She travelled by sea and rail and spent a week in Paris *en route*, staying with her friend Marie-Thérèse Lelio. In Armenia Kar was treated as an honoured guest, and stayed in the comfort of the Hotel Armenia in central Yerevan (Erevan). An exhibition of her Armenian photographs opened in Yerevan on 29 August and was well attended. She returned to London in October.

John Cox became Kar's assistant.

1958 Kar began to photograph regularly for the *Tatler*. In the spring, she travelled to Moscow and then to Sweden. Kar's Armenian photographs were published in her first cover story, 'Return to Armenia', in the *Tatler & Bystander* (8 October).

Kar formally wrote to Kasmin on 14 September asking him to be her manager and the sole agent for her work.

Bryan Robertson, Director of the Whitechapel Art Gallery, wrote to Kar confirming, subject to trustee approval, that Kar would have an exhibition of her work at the Whitechapel in 1960. She photographed Robertson (p.95).

Kar photographed brothers Aldous and Julian Huxley, the writer Han Suyin with her daughter Yung Mei Tang, the architects Maxwell Fry and Jane Drew, George Devine on stage as Hamm in Samuel Beckett's *Endgame* and Patrick Magee in the first production of *Krapp's Last Tape* at the Royal Court Theatre.

1959 Robertson wrote Kar a letter of commendation to encourage prospective sitters in Europe and Russia. Kar photographed Cecil Beaton at his Wiltshire home (p.99), the painter John Bratby with his family in Blackheath (p.101) and Augustus John at home in Hampshire (p.83). Her theatre work included a session with playwright Frank Norman, composer Lionel Bart and actors rehearsing for the musical *Fings Ain't Wot They Used T'Be* at the Theatre Royal, Stratford, East London.

In the summer Kar travelled again to Armenia and in September she visited East Germany, where she documented daily life. An exhibition of her Armenian photographs was held in Berlin in the Zentrale Haus der Deutsch–Sowjetischen Freundschaft (Central House of German–Soviet Friendship). In Moscow, where she travelled with her assistant John Cox, Kar photographed several distinguished sitters, including the composer Dmitri Shostakovich (p.86) and the author Ilya Ehrenburg.

Kar's photo-essay 'A Gallery of Names that Mean Galleries', featuring portraits of gallery-owners and art dealers, was published in the 20 May issue of the *Tatler & Bystander*. The cover story 'The West End Arcadians', with Kar's portraits of shopkeepers and residents of London's arcades, appeared in the 25 November issue. On 9 December 'High Kicks for Low Tension' included Kar's photograph of actress Natasha Parry. The 23 December issue featured photographs of London's Buddhists, Sikhs, Hindus and Muslims to illustrate a piece entitled 'Oriental Religions Among Us'.

Kar's mother died.

1960 Kar's photographs accompanied a *Tatler & Bystander* story called 'Top Level Living' (6 January) about stylish high-rise residents, such as interior designer Gaby Schreiber. Kar travelled to France to photograph sitters for the Whitechapel exhibition, including Georges Braque (pp.84, 140–1), Eugène Ionesco (p.108) and Jack Clemente (p.91).

Following a period of intense preparation, *Ida Kar: An Exhibition of Artists and Writers in Great Britain, France and the Soviet Union* opened at the Whitechapel Art Gallery on 22 March and ran until 1 May. It was the first one-person photographic show to be held in a major London art gallery. Kar received critical acclaim, and her boldly presented work also proved to be a popular success. The exhibition provoked a media debate on the question whether photography is an art form, discussed on the BBC programme *The Critics*, presented by David Sylvester and broadcast on 24 April 1960.

On 27 June Kar appeared in a Pathé newsreel film entitled *Photographer of the Famous* photographing Sir Charles Wheeler, the sculptor and President of the Royal Academy, in his studio. The voiceover noted that exhibitions of Kar's work were winning universal acclaim.

Lionel Bart and Frank Norman, 1959

Gallery-owners Roland, Browse and Delbanco, 1959

51

Victor Musgrave at Gallery One, late 1950s

Anti-nuclear demonstrators including Bertrand Russell, 1961

Billy Fury, 1961

Ida Kar outside the House of Friendship in Moscow, 1962

1961 In April Gallery One moved to 16 North Audley Street in Mayfair. As a member of the Committee of 100, which had been founded the previous year by Bertrand Russell as a more militant strand of the Campaign for Nuclear Disarmament (CND) with 100 public signatories, Kar photographed a demonstration in Whitehall protesting against the agreement to purchase Polaris nuclear submarines from the United States.

Kar photographed her assistant and close friend Terry Taylor listening to jazz records (p.130) and 'around town'. Taylor had lived with Kar and Musgrave at D'Arblay Street for eighteen months in the late 1950s.

Kar's photo-essay 'Men Who Make Music' was published in *Queen* (24 May) and included photographs of William Glock, the BBC's Controller of Music, and Sir Joseph Lockwood, Chairman of EMI. Kar also photographed pop singer Billy Fury at the height of his success.

Kar visited St Ives and photographed the artistic community there. Her photographs of Buster, Terry Frost, Michael Heard, Barbara Hepworth, Patrick Heron, Peter Lanyon, Alan Lowndes, John Milne, Denis Mitchell, Anthony Shiels and Monica Wynter were published as 'Le Quartier St Ives' in the 26 July issue of the *Tatler & Bystander* (pp.116–21).

Kar travelled to the South of France, where she photographed Nadia Khodossevitch-Léger, Fernand Léger's widow. On the return journey by train Kar met the Russian mother of Julieta Preston, who would become her pupil the following year.

1962 Julieta Preston, a photography student, became Kar's pupil and boarder. Preston's role varied greatly; she accompanied Kar on sittings, made prints, and helped with cooking, shopping and entertaining.

Kar was invited to exhibit seventy-six of her Whitechapel prints at Moscow's House of Friendship with Peoples of Foreign Countries. It ran from 2 to 15 April and was very well received both by the public (the exhibition attracted 20,000 visitors) and by the international press. At the 'Festival of Misfits' held at Gallery One in October, Kar photographed participant artist Gustav Metzger (p.134).

Kar took reportage photographs of Joan Littlewood directing actors including Barbara Ferris and James Booth on the set of the film *Sparrows Can't Sing* (1963).

1963 Kar signed a contract with the weekly *Animals* magazine, whose editor-in-chief was the highly successful natural history film-maker Armand Denis. Kar's work appeared in the magazine until 1965. She became enthusiastic about photographing animals, but in an interview also said that after twenty-five years of photographing people she found herself getting terribly depressed. In May the exhibition *Ida Kar: Artist with a Camera* opened at

Ida Kar, Wuppertal Zoo, Germany, 1963

Ida Kar, by Julieta Preston, 1963

Birmingham City Museum and Art Gallery. This included studies of animals, artists and writers. Kar sold a photograph of the Chilean artist Moyano to a Solihull businessman for 60 guineas, the most she had received for a single work.

Following Bridget Riley's second solo exhibition at Gallery One in September (at which Kar photographed the young artist, p.133), Musgrave closed the gallery in North Audley Street in October. Kar and Musgrave moved to 6 Stanhope Place, Bayswater.

1964 At the invitation of the Cuban government, Kar attended celebrations marking the fifth anniversary of the Cuban revolution during a five-week visit beginning in January. There she photographed president Fidel Castro speaking at a televised conference and had sittings with a number of the country's artists and writers, as well as photographing street life in Havana and the surrounding countryside.

Kar photographed the artist Jean Dubuffet 'around town' in Paris and the outsider artist Scottie Wilson going about his daily routine in north-west London.

1964–5 Kar and Musgrave began to spend periods living apart. Kar lived at 18 Palace Gardens, Kensington.

1965 In February, an exhibition of Kar's Cuban photographs ran at the Hamiltons Gallery, Carlos Place, Mayfair for a week before moving to Stepney Central Library.

The Old Man and Ida Kar, **Cuba,** 1964

Fidel Castro, 1964

Ida Kar and Victor Musgrave,
by John Couzins, 1968

Near Boulevard Edgar Quinet, Paris, 1968

Ida Kar, by John Couzins, 22 January 1972

1966 The photo-historian Helmut Gernsheim, a friend and long-term supporter of Kar's work, acquired 124 of her exhibition prints for his collection housed at the University of Texas, where they were shown in October. The Victoria and Albert Museum in London acquired sixteen of Kar's portraits.

1967 Kar and Musgrave moved to 16 Rex Place in Mayfair.

1968 John Couzins became Kar's assistant (and remained so until 1971) in reply to an advertisement Kar had placed in the *British Journal of Photography*. Martin Breese became one of Kar's last assistants.

In March Kar exhibited at the Foyle House Gallery, Midland Arts Centre, Birmingham alongside photographers including Bill Brandt, whom she photographed in August.

Kar went to live in Paris for several weeks, intending to take documentary photographs. There she sang with the Salvation Army, who helped her financially. Suffering increasingly from bipolar disorder, Kar was admitted to a psychiatric hospital, but still managed to produce a photographic record of her stay in the city.

1969 Kar and Musgrave separated and left Rex Place. Kar settled in a bedsit at Flat 2, 47 Inverness Terrace, London W2. Kar's Armenian heritage became increasingly important to her, and she attended services at St Sarkis, the Armenian Orthodox Church in Iverna Gardens, Kensington.

1970s Despite worsening mental health, Kar remained committed to photography, beginning a project to photograph nudes in a makeshift studio in her bedsit. In November 1974 Kar received the two enlarged prints of these, which she had ordered the previous month. Kar began to record her autobiography on tapes which are now lost.

1974 Ida Kar died alone in her home following a cerebral haemorrhage on 24 December.

1981 The National Portrait Gallery acquired twenty vintage prints by Ida Kar from Dorothy Bohm at the Photographer's Gallery on behalf of Victor Musgrave. In December the Metropolitan Museum of Art, New York accepted a gift of Kar's photograph of Brassaï, donated by Victor Musgrave.

1982 Kasmin held an exhibition of sixty vintage photographs by Ida Kar at the Knoedler Kasmin Gallery, Cork Street, London in December. Twelve prints were sold at prices ranging from £72 to £125. The exhibition travelled to the Scottish Gallery, Edinburgh and Aberdeen Art Gallery.

1984 Victor Musgrave died.

1988 Kar was included in the *Women by Women* display and calendar – the National Portrait Gallery's contribution to Spectrum, the Women's Photography Festival held in October.

1989 Val Williams' monograph *Ida Kar: Photographer 1908–1974* was published by Virago Press. An exhibition of Kar's work was held at Zelda Cheatle Gallery, London from 13 to 31 October.

1993 Six of Kar's portraits were included in the exhibition, *A Second Look: Women Photographers from the Collections of the Harry Ransom Humanities Research Centre*, Austin, Texas from 22 March to 25 July.

1996 Kar's portrait of Cecil Beaton was used on the poster of the exhibition *The Room in View* at the National Portrait Gallery from 23 February to 2 June.

1999 The National Portrait Gallery purchased the Ida Kar archive, comprising 800 photographic prints, 10,000 negatives, 400 vintage contact prints, exhibition catalogues, correspondence with sitters and press cuttings. The archive had previously been in the care of Monika Kinley, Musgrave's partner, with whom he had established the Musgrave Kinley Outsider Art Collection in 1981. The collection is now held by the Whitworth Art Gallery at the University of Manchester.

2011 The exhibition *Ida Kar: Bohemian Photographer, 1908–1974* is held at the National Portrait Gallery from 10 March to 19 June.

PLATES

EARLY YEARS IN LONDON

58

1 Tutte Lemkow, 1952

2 **Sylvia Syms,** 1953

60

3 Jacob Epstein, 1953

4 Bertrand Russell, 1953

FORTY ARTISTS FROM LONDON AND PARIS

5 **Henry Moore,** 1954

6 **Ivon Hitchens,** 1954

7 **Stanley Spencer,** 1954

8 **Kenneth Armitage,** 1954

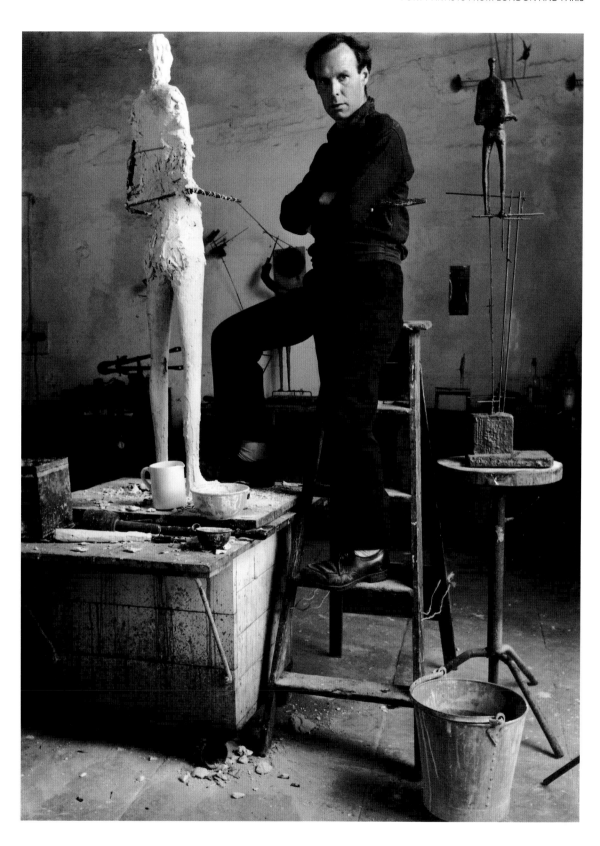

9 **Reg Butler,** 1954

69

10 **John Piper,** 1954

11 **Kathleen and Graham Sutherland,** 1954

12 **Fernand Léger**, 1954

13 **Marc Chagall,** 1954

14 **Man Ray,** 1954

15 **Marie Laurencin,** 1954

16 **Le Corbusier,** 1954

17 **Gino Severini**, 1954

18 **Germaine Richier,** 1954

19 **Alberto Giacometti,** 1954

78

20 **Tsugouharu Foujita,** 1954

21 Camille Bombois with his wife, Eugénie Christophe, 1954

THE ART WORLD

22 **Yves Klein**, 1957

23 **Feliks Topolski,** 1950s

24 **Augustus John,** 1959

25 **Georges Braque**, 1960

26 **Jean Arp,** 1960

86

27 **Dmitri Shostakovich,** 1959

28 **Ossip Zadkine,** 1954

88

29 **Sandra Blow,** 1955

30 **F.N. Souza,** 1958

31 **Alexander Weatherson,** 1958

32 **Jack Clemente**, 1960

33 **Hussein Shariffe,** 1960

34 **Keith Vaughan,** 1960

94

35 **John Kasmin**, 1959

36 **Bryan Robertson,** 1958

96

37 **Erica Brausen,** 1959

38 **Helen Lessore,** 1959

'Many thanks for sending the pictures which I think are very good indeed ... I was a bit surprised at first to see myself standing in such a stiff strange way. It is unlike any other photograph of me. I suppose it is an interesting slant – a development. It was stupid of me not to put the hat on with more of a dash.'

'What a good photographer you are! I am always discovering that the picture I like is taken by you ... If I can be of any help in the future in some small way, do call on me.'

Cecil Beaton

39 **Cecil Beaton,** 1960

40 **Bernard Kops with his wife, Erica, and their son, Adam,** 1960

41 **John Bratby with his wife, Jean Cooke, and their son, David,** 1959

PORTRAITS OF WRITERS

42 **Colin MacInnes**, 1957

104

43 **Laurie Lee,** 1956

44 **Doris Lessing,** 1958

45 **Samuel Selvon,** 1956

107

46 **Iris Murdoch,** 1957

47 **Eugène Ionesco,** 1960

48 **Jean-Paul Sartre,** 1961

49 **Helmut Gernsheim,** 1962

50 **André Breton,** 1960

51 **Royston Ellis,** 1960

52 **Laura Del Rivo**, 1961

53 **T.S. Eliot,** 1959

54 **Somerset Maugham**, 1958

LE QUARTIER ST IVES

55 **Barbara Hepworth,** 1961

118

56 **Patrick Heron**, 1961

57 **John Milne,** 1961

120

58 **Terry Frost,** 1961

59 **Peter Lanyon with his daughter, Anne-Marie,** 1961

DOCUMENTARY PORTRAITS

60 **State lottery, Stalinstadt,** 1959

61 **Boys at the indoor market, Yerevan,** 1957

124

62 **Juan Arcocha, Havana,** 1964

63 **Hugo Consuegra with his wife, Rita Arias, Havana, 1964**

64 **Alberto Korda, Havana,** 1964

65 *Taking a Breeze in Old Havana,* 1964

THE LONDON SCENE AND LATER SITTINGS

66 **Maggie Smith,** 1961

67 **Terry Taylor,** 1961

68 **Brian Robins** (1928–88) **with his wife, Susan,** 1960

'Her [Bridget Riley's] second exhibition at Gallery One, 16 North Audley Street, involves one's whole sense of stability and physical confidence by launching one assault after another on what the eye tries to accept as taut geometric order.'

The Times, 30 September 1963

69 **Bridget Riley**, 1963

70 **Gustav Metzger,** 1962

71 **John Latham**, 1963

72 **Oskar Rabine with his wife, Valentina Kropivnitskaya, and their son, Alexandre,** 1962

73 Paul Millichip with his wife, Felicity Evershed, and their children, Diana and Robin, 1960

138

74 **Bill Brandt,** 1968

75 **Mother and child,** 1974

Georges Braque, vintage contact sheet, 1961

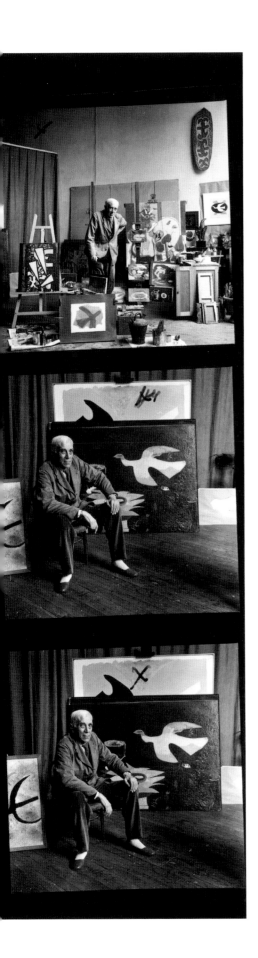

NOTES ON PLATES
GEORGIA ATIENZA
CLARE FREESTONE

EARLY YEARS IN LONDON

1 Tutte Lemkow (1918–91)
1952
Norwegian-born Lemkow moved to England in 1946 with his first wife, the actress Mai Zetterling. He pursued a career in ballet, but went on to play small parts in films, starting with *The Lost People* (1949), in which Zetterling starred. Lemkow appeared on the London stage in comedies such as *Thieves' Carnival* (1952), and had numerous dance roles in films including *Moulin Rouge* (1952) and *The Captain's Paradise* (1953). He established himself by playing eccentric foreigners in war films, comedies and thrillers, as well as choreographing dance sequences for both film and television. Kar's portrait of Lemkow was taken in her studio above Gallery One on Litchfield Street at a time when she worked as a theatrical photographer; many of her commissions appeared in the stage and screen casting directory *Spotlight*.

2 Sylvia Syms (b.1934)
1953
Syms studied at the Royal Academy of Dramatic Art and appeared in her first film aged nineteen. *My Teenage Daughter* (1954), in which she starred alongside Anna Neagle, was Syms' first major screen appearance and was followed by nine more films in the 1950s, including *Ice-Cold in Alex* (1958) and the English Civil War story *Moonraker* (1958). Syms' long career has encompassed notable film performances, including *The Tamarind Seed* (1974); radio performances; directing her own theatre company, Words & Music; and recently a role in the BBC television soap opera *EastEnders*. Kar photographed Syms as she embarked on her acting career, the year before her stage debut in George Bernard Shaw's *The Apple Cart* at the Theatre Royal, Haymarket. Kar achieved the intense lighting in this publicity portrait using two PhotoFlood lights with reflectors.

3 Jacob Epstein (1880–1959)
1953
Born in New York to Polish-Jewish parents, Epstein studied in Paris (1902–3) before moving to London in 1905. He quickly gained a reputation for his brilliant carvings, sculpted monuments and portraits, and controversial depictions of nudity. He had his first solo show at the Twenty-One Gallery in 1913 and became known as an advocate of modernist sculpture as well as vigorous realism. Epstein met Kathleen Garman in 1921 and they formed a lasting relationship, having three children together: Theo, Kitty and Esther. It wasn't until late in life that Epstein received public recognition (he was knighted in 1954) for works such as *Lazarus* (1947–8) and *Social Consciousness* (1951–3), and despite ill health and grieving for the deaths of two of his children in 1954, Epstein completed eight large public commissions in his last decade, as well as many commissioned portraits. It was during this period, while Kar was acting as guardian for Theo, that she photographed Epstein at 18 Park Gate, Kensington, along with his works in progress, such as *Madonna and Child* (1953) before its installation at Cavendish Square, celebrity portrait sittings (opposite) and Kathleen and their children.

4 Bertrand Russell (1872–1970)
1953
Russell's contributions to logic, epistemology and mathematics established him as one of the foremost philosophers of the twentieth century. He was awarded the Nobel Prize for Literature in 1950 in recognition of his liberal and humanitarian writings. Russell, who was closely associated with the Bloomsbury group, consolidated his reputation as a philosopher with the *Principia Mathematica* (1910–13). A committed pacifist, in 1958 Russell became the first president of the Campaign for Nuclear Disarmament (CND) and in 1960 went on to form the more militant Committee of 100, advocating non-violent civil disobedience to achieve their aims. Kar became a member of the Committee of 100 and photographed a sit-down demonstration in Whitehall protesting against the agreement to purchase Polaris nuclear submarines from the USA. In 1953 Kar used a photograph of Russell and Epstein (opposite) for her Christmas card.

FORTY ARTISTS FROM LONDON AND PARIS

Ida Kar took the portraits in this section, or variants from the same sitting, to her exhibition *Forty Artists from London and Paris*, which ran at Gallery One in London's Litchfield Street from 12 to 31 October 1954.

5 **Henry Moore** (1898–1986)
1954

Born in Yorkshire, the son of a miner, Moore studied at Leeds School of Art and the Royal College of Art, later teaching there until 1932. He participated in the avant-garde groups the Seven and Five Society and Unit One, and in the international surrealist exhibitions in London (1936) and Paris (1938). In 1948 Moore won the International Sculpture Prize at the Venice Biennale and was one of the featured artists at the Festival of Britain (1951) and Germany's documenta 1 (1955). This photograph dates from Kar's first visit to Moore's studio at Much Hadham in Hertfordshire. The sculptor wrote to Kar the following year regarding a request by *Vogue* to use this image in their November 1955 issue to publicise Moore's Leicester Galleries exhibition of 'ten important pieces of recent sculpture shown for the first time: typically powerful, with a sense of driving muscle and no fleshiness', saying 'I am very pleased that [*Vogue*] want to do it full-page.' Kar photographed Moore with two casts of *Family Group* (1949), an earlier version of which was his first large-scale commission for a bronze.

6 **Ivon Hitchens** (1893–1979)
1954

Hitchens studied at the Royal Academy Schools before being elected a member of the influential Seven and Five Society of modern British artists. Hitchens's first solo exhibition was held at the Mayor Gallery in London in 1925, but from 1940 to 1960 he was represented by the Leicester Galleries and later by the Waddington Galleries. In 1940 Hitchens, his wife, Mollie, and baby son, John (who also later became a painter), moved from Hampstead to Greenleaves, Petworth, Sussex, where he was able to develop his mature style of semi-abstract, richly coloured paintings undisturbed. Enjoying the Hitchens' warm hospitality and friendship, Kar visited on numerous occasions, often with her assistant, John Cox, taking portraits of the family. Following this photograph, taken in August 1954, Mollie Hitchens wrote to Kar, 'Your photos arrived safely this morning and we really are highly delighted with them.'

143

7 **Stanley Spencer** (1891–1959)
1954

Spencer commuted back to his childhood home in Cookham-on-Thames, Berkshire, while studying at the Slade School of Fine Art, London (1907–12) alongside Paul Nash and Mark Gertler. Here his small stature and pudding-bowl haircut ensured that Spencer stood out from the crowd. Following his studies, Spencer's paintings began to demonstrate his strong religious convictions and, after enlisting in the Royal Army Medical Corps during the First World War, he developed an interest in the human body. Spencer's most noted works include *The Resurrection, Cookham* (1924–6), depicting his love for his first wife, Hilda, and *Double Nude Portrait: The Artist and His Second Wife* (1937). Following his work as an official war artist during the Second World War, Spencer returned to Cookham, where he became an increasingly eccentric character. He was elected a Royal Academician in 1950, and in 1955, the year after Kar photographed Spencer with the umbrella which accompanied him wherever he went, he was honoured with a major retrospective at the Tate Gallery. Spencer was knighted in 1959, shortly before his death. Kar's portrait of Spencer was used for the front cover of Maurice Collis's biography of the artist published in 1962.

8 **Kenneth Armitage** (1916–2002)
1954

Armitage was born in Leeds, where he studied at the College of Art before attending the Slade School of Fine Art in London (1937–9). After serving in the army during the Second World War, he was appointed Head of Sculpture at Bath Academy of Art, Corsham, a post he held for ten years. Kar photographed Armitage at his Earls Court flat, with *Linked Figures* (1949), modelled with plaster over netting, and *Standing Group 2* (1952), one of his screen-like groups. Around this time Armitage developed his style of abstraction based on a simplification of the human form. Armitage was included in the influential exhibition *New Aspects of British Sculpture* at the Venice Biennale in 1952, and in 1958 was selected for the Biennale's David E. Bright Prize for a sculptor under the age of forty-five. Armitage wrote to Kar regarding her Gallery One show: 'I'm sure your exhibition will prove a real success.'

9 **Reg Butler** (1913–81)
1954

Although Butler trained as an architect, by 1937 his interests had turned to sculpture. His first solo show was in 1949 at the Hanover Gallery in London, and two years later he was awarded the Gregory Fellowship in sculpture at the University of Leeds. In 1951 he was commissioned to produce a work for the Festival of Britain and was appointed as a teacher at the Slade School of Fine Art. By this point Butler was considered one of Britain's leading sculptors, a central figure in the group that represented what Herbert Read termed the 'geometry of fear'. The high point of his career came in 1954, when he won a competition arranged by the Institute for Contemporary Arts to produce a sculpture of the *Unknown Political Prisoner*. Ida Kar photographed Butler in his Berkhamsted studio while he was working on *Manipulator*, one of his few sculptures to depict a male figure. During this period his work was typified by the use of forged and welded metals to produce brutal sculptures that were representative of post-war anxiety. In a letter to Kar, Butler wrote that the selected photographs were 'splendid', apart from the rings under his eyes.

10 **John Piper** (1903–92)
1954

Piper studied at the Royal College of Art before becoming a member of the avant-garde Seven and Five Society and, from 1934, developing abstract reliefs and beginning a collaboration with writer and librettist Myfanwy Evans (whom he married in 1937) on the magazine *Axis*. Piper gained prominence for a representational style as well as for his stage designs, notably for Benjamin Britten, with whom Piper first collaborated on the opera *The Rape of Lucretia* (1946). Piper, who had a versatile creative talent, worked with John Betjeman on the *Shell Guides* and was a skilled printmaker. In the year before Kar photographed him, Piper began his association with the stained-glass maker Patrick Reyntiens, producing windows for Oundle College chapel (1953–6) and the baptistery window (1957–62) in Basil Spence's new Coventry Cathedral. Kar photographed Piper at Fawley Bottom Farmhouse, Oxford where he lived from 1935. He is shown with a stage design and his painting *Stone Gate, Portland* (1950), a coastal view that Piper depicted more often than any other landscape. Myfanwy Piper's letter to Kar making the arrangements for this sitting in July ('we are away until Thursday and then have 3 hard days' work here …') demonstrates the active schedules for which the Pipers were known.

11 **Kathleen** (1905–91) and **Graham** (1903–80) **Sutherland**
1954

Graham Sutherland studied at Goldsmith's College of Art (1921–6) and worked mainly as an engraver until 1930. In 1927, while teaching at Chelsea School of Art, he married Kathleen Barry, a fashion student. Sutherland made his reputation as a painter of Romantic abstract landscapes, and in 1938, with the patronage of Sir Kenneth Clark, he presented his first one-man show. From 1940 Sutherland was employed as an official artist in the Second World War, as part of the War Artists' Scheme. In the 1940s and 1950s he painted many acclaimed portraits, including those of Somerset Maugham (1949) and Sir Winston Churchill (1954). The latter was controversially destroyed on Lady Churchill's orders. Kar photographed the Sutherlands, an intensely close couple, in their home, the White House, in Trottiscliffe, Kent. Over the fireplace stand studies from Sutherland's series of *Thorn Trees* and *Thorn Heads*, images that developed from his preoccupation with the Crucifixion. Writing to Ida Kar from La Villa Blanche in Menton in France in 1959, Kathleen Sutherland commented, 'You certainly know how to get the best out of people and we'll remember liking the [photographs] you took of us better than anyone else's!'

12 **Fernand Léger** (1881–1955)
1954

Léger was born into a peasant family in Argentan, France. He studied in Paris at the School of Decorative Arts and at the Académie Julian. A retrospective of Cézanne's work at the Paris Salon d'Automne in 1907, and the recent experiments of cubism, influenced the development of Léger's own style. In 1908 he rented a studio at the artists' colony La Ruche (The Beehive), and the following year developed a semi-abstract cubist idiom, breaking down forms into tubular shapes. Following his service in the First World War, his work demonstrated a fascination with man and machine, depicting geometric and mechanised figures. In the 1920s, influenced by the formalist movement purism, Léger used muted colours and bold, black outlines in his work. He also collaborated on the experimental film *The Mechanical Ballet* (1924), designed sets and costumes for ballet productions and worked on large decorative commissions. Bill Hopkins wrote of this portrait: 'Standing beside one of his latest still lifes, Léger's virtuosity has caused as many controversies in painting as Stravinsky in music. Looking at him, he is the Norman farmer epitomised. Not what one regards a revolutionary at all.' That same year Léger completed one of his final works, *The Great Parade*, which depicts the leisure activities of the working classes.

13 Marc Chagall (1887–1985)
1954
Chagall was born in Vitebsk, Russia, into an observant Jewish family. In 1907 he moved to St Petersburg, where he studied painting for three years, eventually under the tutelage of the stage designer Léon Bakst. In 1910 Chagall moved to Paris, settling in the bohemian colony La Ruche (The Beehive). There he met avant-garde poets including Blaise Cendrars and Guillaume Apollinaire and young artists such as Robert Delaunay and Fernand Léger. In 1911 he exhibited at the Salon des Artistes Indépendants, and in 1914 had his first one-man exhibition in Berlin before returning to Russia. Chagall's work presented dreamlike subject matter in rich colours, and his imagery, drawn partly from memories of his early years, included flying lovers, fantastic animals, biblical prophets and fiddlers on roofs. After the Russian Revolution he was appointed commissar for art in the province of Vitebsk and directed an art academy. In 1923 Chagall settled again in Paris, this time with his wife and daughter. His autobiography *Ma Vie* was published in 1930. Chagall was a prolific painter and also worked as book illustrator, designer of stained glass and mosaics, and did sets and costumes for ballet and opera productions. This photograph of Chagall was used to advertise Kar's 1954 exhibition at Gallery One in London.

14 Man Ray (1890–1976)
1954
Born Emmanuel Radnitzky in Philadelphia, Pennsylvania, Man Ray grew up in New York. In 1915 he met the French artist Marcel Duchamp, and together they formed the New York group of Dada artists. In 1921 Man Ray moved to Paris, where he played a key role in the Dada and surrealist movements, producing paintings, assemblage-objects, films and photographs. He pioneered new photographic techniques such as 'rayographs' and 'solarizations' and was active as a portrait and fashion photographer for *Vogue* and *Vanity Fair* in the 1920s and *Harper's Bazaar* in the 1930s. Kar photographed Man Ray at his Paris apartment-studio at 2 bis rue Férou, near the Luxembourg Gardens, where he moved in 1952 with wife and muse Juliet Browner. He appears posing next to *Mademoiselle H.* (1952), a portrait of a young friend called Henriette that hung at Man Ray's home until his death.

15 Marie Laurencin (1883/5–1956)
1954
Laurencin trained at the Humbert Academy in Paris, where she studied alongside Georges Braque. She became associated with Picasso and Apollinaire and the artists working at Bateau-Lavoir in Montmartre, exhibiting for the first time in 1907 at the Salon des Indépendants. In 1908 Laurencin sold her first painting, *Group of Artists*, to Gertrude Stein. It depicted herself, Apollinaire, Picasso and Fernande Olivier. Laurencin is best known for her delicate and stylised dark-eyed female figures in pastel colours. She also worked as a set designer for Diaghilev's production of Poulenc's ballet *Les Biches* (1924) and illustrated numerous books, including

a French edition of Lewis Carroll's *Alice's Adventures in Wonderland* (1930). This portrait of Laurencin was taken at her home in the Forest of Sénart, near Paris, two years before she died.

16 Le Corbusier (1887–1965)
1954
Charles-Edouard Jeanneret, known as Le Corbusier, was born in La Chaux-de-Fonds, Switzerland. Widely acclaimed as the most influential architect of the twentieth century, Le Corbusier was also a celebrated writer and artist. In 1917 he met the painter and designer Amédée Ozenfant, and together they developed purism, an aesthetic of simple geometric forms. In 1920 they founded *L'Esprit Nouveau*, a magazine that proposed functionalist ideas in architecture and city planning. Le Corbusier's architecture and innovative thinking revolutionised modern living with designs that ranged from private villas to large-scale social housing developments and utopian urban plans. His ideas still resonate in contemporary architecture. Key works include the Citrohan House (1922), Unite d'Habitation in Marseilles (1946–52), Notre Dame du Haut, Ronchamp, France (1950–5), the city complex of Chandigarh, India (1950–6) and the National Museum of Western Art, Tokyo (1960). Kar photographed Le Corbusier at his Paris studio situated on the seventh floor of 24 rue Nungesser et Coli, where he moved in 1934. He is pictured at work with some of his still lifes behind him.

17 Gino Severini (1883–1966)
1954
Severini was born in Cortona in Tuscany. He moved to Rome in 1899 and briefly studied drawing at the Villa Medici. Giacomo Balla, who later became a prominent futurist, introduced Severini to Seurat's divisionism, where colours on the canvas are mixed by the eye, a technique Severini continued to use during his cubist and futurist periods. He settled in Paris in 1906, meeting Braque, Picasso and other leading artists. In 1910 Severini signed the futurist manifesto and played an important role in exporting futurism to the Parisian avant-garde. In 1913 Severini had his first one-man exhibition at the Marlborough Gallery, London. Later in his career he worked on numerous decorative panels, frescoes and mosaics, and designed sets and costumes for the theatre. His writings include *Du cubisme au classicisme* (1921) and an autobiography, *Tutta la vita di un pittore* (*The Life of a Painter*, 1946). Of this portrait, taken at Severini's atelier in the town of Meudon near Paris, Bill Hopkins wrote that 'every morning on arriving at his studio, he [Severini] takes off his bowler hat and rolls himself a paper hat from the day's newspaper. On the morning this photograph was taken he was advertising Sir Winston Churchill's memoirs on his forehead.'

18 Germaine Richier (1902–59)
1954
Richier studied at the École des Beaux Arts in Montpellier and with the sculptor Antoine Bourdelle in Paris (1926–9). Richier's approach was classical but her themes were fantastical,

combining human and animal forms from 1940. In 1934 Richier had her first solo exhibition in Paris. Her post-war sculptures, such as *Hurricane Woman* (1948–9), with which she appears in Kar's portrait, can be read as expressions of humanity under threat. Bill Hopkins wrote that 'The sculpting of a subject's atmosphere – in this case controlled violence – is the outstanding factor in her success as a "realist" … Germaine Richier is that phenomenon – a successful woman in sculpture. Meeting her, one senses a masculine objectivity married to an ultra-femininity, that most particular property of Parisians.' Richier married the art critic René de Solier in the year of this portrait and the following year had a major exhibition at London's Hanover Gallery. Writing about this portrait, taken in the sitter's Paris studio, Kar noted 'I was struck by the extraordinary resemblance of her figure next to her work, and simply recorded it.'

19 **Alberto Giacometti** (1901–66)
1954

Swiss-born Giacometti moved to Paris in 1922, where he studied until 1925 under the sculptor Emile-Antoine Bourdelle. In 1926 Giacometti made his first cubist sculptures, and in the late 1920s, at the same time as Kar was living in Paris, he became influenced by surrealism and joined the movement in 1930. Giacometti had his first solo show in 1932, and in the late 1930s his figurative sculptures became very small. It was his post-war work, including the tall figures of 1947–8, that secured his reputation. In the same year in which Kar photographed Giacometti, his second exhibition at Galerie Maeght in Paris was accompanied by an essay by his friend, the exponent of existentialism Jean-Paul Sartre. Also in 1954, Giacometti designed sets for Samuel Beckett's *Waiting for Godot* and the writer Jean Genet posed for him. In 1956 Giacometti's sculptures of female standing figures were shown at the Venice Biennale, where in 1962 he was awarded the grand prize for sculpture. This photograph was taken on the steps of Giacometti's studio at 46 rue Hippolyte-Maindron, Montparnasse, where he had lived and worked since 1927.

20 **Tsugouharu Foujita** (1886–1968)
1954

The Japanese artist Foujita moved to Montparnasse in Paris in 1913. There he frequented artists' cafes, became friends with Picasso and Matisse and was acquainted with Modigliani, Soutine and Léger. Man Ray's model Kiki was a frequent visitor to his first studio and posed for the painter. His work married Eastern and Western styles and by the mid-1920s had been exhibited worldwide. Foujita returned to Paris after spending the war years in Japan. In 1955 he became a French citizen and he converted to Catholicism in 1959. Bill Hopkins wrote of Kar's photograph of the sixty-eight-year-old artist, 'Foujita's delicacy of line and colour gives the only clue to his curious passion for puppets, which he claims he "loves beyond all human beings". Here he is surrounded by them; many of them are period curios.' Photographed with a quarter-plate camera, this portrait was enlarged to 48 x 39 inches when a print was later shown at the Whitechapel.

21 **Camille Bombois** (1883–1966) **with his wife, Eugénie Christophe**
1954

Born in Venarey-les-Laumes in the Côte d'Or in eastern France, Bombois grew up on a canal barge. At the age of twelve he was sent to work on a farm. Known for his strength, he became a local champion wrestler and joined a travelling circus. From 1907 Bombois lived in Paris, working as a labourer. He later took a night job at a newspaper printing press and painted during the day, making several visits to the Louvre to study the old masters. He served in the First World War and received several awards for bravery. By 1922 his pavement displays in Montmartre had come to the attention of Wilhelm Uhde and other critics. Bombois soon became one of the best-known naïve painters of his day, participating in numerous collective exhibitions. He had his first one-man show in 1944 at the Galerie Pétridès in Paris. Kar photographed Bombois with his wife Eugénie Christophe at their home in the suburbs of the city. A variant pose of Bombois next to one of his circus paintings was included in Kar's 1954 Gallery One exhibition. Bill Hopkins wrote: 'Still the honest, down-to earth peasant, Bombois's one concession to his fame is the velvet poet's tie.'

THE ART WORLD

22 **Yves Klein** (1928–62)
1957

Born in Nice, into a family of artists, Klein began to paint in the late 1940s. He lived in Japan from 1952 to 1953, where he became an expert at judo, which he later taught in Spain and Paris, his home from 1955. He is best known for his monochrome works and expressed his theories in several manifestos, stating in 1955: 'In this way I seek to individualize the colour, because I have come to believe that there is a living world of each colour and I express these worlds.' Klein's early monochromes were in orange, yellow, pink, red and green. From 1957 he worked mainly in blue, which he later patented as International Klein Blue. His exhibition *Monochrome Propositions of Yves Klein*, held at Gallery One in London in 1957, caused great controversy. The press ran stories with headlines such as 'The Artist who Paints Nothing' (*Daily Mirror*, 25 June 1957) and 'An Artist with The Blues. Reductio Ad Absurdum' (*The Times*, 12 July 1957). Kar photographed Klein next to one of his 'blue sponge' sculptures at Gallery One.

23 **Feliks Topolski** (1907–89)
1950s

Topolski studied at the Warsaw Academy of Art (1927–32) and travelled widely before moving to London in 1935 and establishing a studio in Little Venice, where he and his actress wife entertained writers, artists and politicians. His graphic style made his work well suited to use as illustrations, and during the Second World War his reputation in Britain as a gifted draughtsman saw him appointed as an official war artist. In 1951 he painted a mural for the Festival of Britain, creating it in an arch beneath Hungerford Bridge near Waterloo Station, and in 1953, commissioned by the Duke of Edinburgh, he was official artist at the Coronation of Queen

Elizabeth II. Topolski began producing his illustrated *Chronicle* broadsheets, a self-printed fortnightly publication combining text and illustrations, in the year before Kar photographed him. Popular success followed with his portraits for the BBC television series *Face to Face* (1959–62) and a series of twenty portraits in 1961–2 of literary figures. Kar photographed Topolski in his Hungerford Bridge studio ('a magical space … a huge printing press and paintings, drawings, prints and papers piled high'). The portrait in the photograph may be of the pregnant wife of Topolski's friend Brian Chen.

24 **Augustus John** (1878–1961)
1959

John studied at the Slade School of Art together with his sister, the painter Gwen John. By the age of twenty he had gained a reputation as one of the most brilliant draughtsmen in England, winning numerous awards. From 1901 to 1904 he taught painting at the University of Liverpool and travelled throughout Europe and the USA. John became a leading figure of the avant-garde in the Edwardian period and was noted for his flamboyant personality. He excelled at portraiture, particularly depictions of his friends and fellow artists, and is also noted for his paintings of gypsies and coastal scenes. This photograph was taken during a visit to John's studio in Fryern Court, near Fordingbridge, Hampshire, and was first exhibited at the Whitechapel Art Gallery. Nicholas Elam reviewed Kar's exhibition in *Oxford Opinion* (May 1960), and of this portrait noted that 'Augustus John, his fame and bearing that of an old man but his expression intense and aware, [is] determined not to miss a second of the life that remains.'

25 **Georges Braque** (1882–1963)
1960

Braque grew up in Le Havre, where in 1899 he was apprenticed to a painter-decorator. After attending the *École Supérieure d'Art* in Le Havre, Braque went to Paris to continue his training, studying at the Académie Humbert. In 1905–07 he painted landscapes in the fauve style, using bright colours and impulsive brushwork. The year 1907 marked an aesthetic change in Braque's work, possibly influenced by Paul Cézanne's memorial exhibition at the Salon d'Automne and by his meeting with Picasso, in whose studio he saw *Les demoiselles d'Avignon*. These two events contributed to a transition towards a more subtle palette and a fragmentation of form in Braque's work. During the summer of 1908 he painted radically innovative canvases, a series of landscapes including *Houses at L'Estaque* which were described by Matisse as 'little cubes', anticipating cubist geometric forms. His friendship and partnership with Picasso would lead to the joint creation of cubism. Kar photographed Braque at his Paris studio, at a time when he was working on the *Birds* series. His experimentations with silhouettes and ideograms, carved into painted plaster plaques or on pebbles he picked up on the shore at Varengeville-sur-Mer, led to him producing lithographic works such as *Oiseau de feu* (*Firebird*, 1958) and *Oiseau en vol* (*Bird in Flight*, 1961).

26 **Jean Arp** (1886–1966)
1960

Hans Arp, later Jean, trained in his native Strasbourg, and subsequently studied in Weimar and at the Académie Julian in Paris. In 1912 he met Sonia and Robert Delaunay in Paris, and Kandinsky and the artists of the Blaue Reiter group in Munich. At the beginning of the First World War he moved to Zurich, where he made his first monochrome wood reliefs and was a co-founder of the Dada movement in 1916. From 1919 to 1920 he collaborated in Dada activities with Max Ernst in Cologne before moving to Paris. He contributed to the periodical *La révolution surréaliste* and showed his work at the first exhibition of surrealist artists in 1925. After 1928, he developed his best-known work, the sculptures 'in the round'. In 1930 he made his first *papiers déchirés* (torn papers) and the following year participated in the Abstraction-Création movement. He continued his experiments with abstract form and also wrote poetry. In 1954, he was awarded the Grand Prize for Sculpture at the Venice Biennale. Kar photographed Arp at his studio, now the Arp Foundation, 21 rue des Châtaigniers in Clamart, near Paris, with sculptures including *Tree of Bowls* (1947) and *Torse de Muse* (1959). During the later years of his life, Arp divided his time between a studio in Locarno, Switzerland, where he lived with his second wife, and his home in Clamart, which was designed by his first wife, the artist Sophie Taeuber.

27 **Dmitri Shostakovich** (1906–75)
1959

One of the most celebrated composers of the twentieth century, Shostakovich was born in St Petersburg. The son of an engineer, he entered the Petrograd Conservatory at the age of thirteen, studying piano and composition. His graduation piece, *Symphony No. 1* (1924–5), premiered in 1926 to international acclaim. At the following year's Chopin International Competition for Pianists, in Warsaw, Shostakovich received an honourable mention, despite suffering from appendicitis. His works include symphonies and string quartets (fifteen of each), three completed operas, two concertos each for piano, cello and violin, chamber works and piano music, as well as ballets, songs, jazz suites and almost forty film scores. Throughout his life he struggled to reconcile his creativity with the demands of government-imposed standards for Soviet art. In preparation for her 1960 Whitechapel exhibition, Kar photographed Shostakovich in the Soviet Union in 1959. That year he wrote his First Cello Concerto, for Rostropovich, and saw the premieres of his operetta *Moscow Cheryomushki*, his re-orchestration of Musorgsky's *Boris Godunov* and a film version of Musorgsky's opera *Khovanshchina*, which he completed and for which he co-wrote the screenplay.

28 **Ossip Zadkine** (1890–1967)
1954

Russian-born to a Scottish mother, Zadkine first visited England in 1905. He later returned to study sculpture at London's Regent Street Polytechnic and at the Central School of Arts and Crafts, before settling in Paris in 1909. He practised direct carving in wood and stone and made simplified figures, influenced by Romanesque art and, later, by cubism. Kar photographed Zadkine in his Parisian studio, 100 bis rue d'Assas (now the Musée Zadkine), next to one of his best-known works, *The Destroyed City* (1948–51), a memorial to the 1940 bombing of Rotterdam by the Germans. During the 1940s Zadkine experimented by perforating the sculptures with apertures. He was awarded the grand prize for sculpture at the Venice Biennale (1950).

29 **Sandra Blow** (1925–2006)
1955

Blow began her art education at St Martin's School of Art in London aged just fifteen, followed by spells at the Royal Academy Schools (1946–7) and the Academy of Fine Arts in Rome (1947–8). By the mid-1940s Blow was familiar with Soho's bohemian nightlife and at the time Kar and Musgrave were establishing themselves in London, she had become acquainted with the artists congregating there. While Blow was travelling in 1947, the Italian abstract artist Alberto Burri became her lover and inspired her to adopt, from 1956, the techniques of abstraction and collage. Blow had her first solo exhibition at the Gimpel Fils Gallery in London in 1951 and exhibited there throughout the following decade, developing her paintings of natural space and material surfaces. In 1957 she featured in the first John Moores biannual exhibition in Liverpool (she won second prize there in 1961) and was included in the Young Artists section at the Venice Biennale in 1958. Blow went to stay with the artist Patrick Heron and lived in St Ives for a time (1957–8), making frequent visits over the following years. From 1960 to 1975 she taught at the Royal College of Art and was elected a Royal Academician in 1978.

30 **F.N. Souza** (1924–2002)
1958

Souza had a Catholic upbringing in Goa and studied at the Sir J. J. (Jamsetjee Jeejebhoy) School of Art, Bombay (Mumbai). He was a founding member of the Progressive Artists Group, encouraging Indian artists to participate in art internationally. In 1949 he left India for London. Souza received little recognition until 1954, when Stephen Spender's magazine *Encounter* published his autobiographical essay 'Nirvana of a Maggot' and he was included in a group show at the Institute of Contemporary Arts, where Victor Musgrave became aware of his work. Gallery One held Souza's first solo (sell-out) show in February 1955 and John Berger's review of Souza's 'interesting and puzzling' figurative work, which commented on its expressionist and *art brut* influences, gave a further boost to the artist's career. Gallery One continued to represent Souza, giving him five solo shows between 1956 and 1961, the last of which was held at the North Audley Street premises, where his larger paintings could be displayed. In a contemporary review in *Apollo* Souza was quoted as saying, 'I leave discretion, understatement, and discrimination to the finicky and lunatic fringe.' Kar photographed Souza on several occasions – once with his third wife and baby. He is

shown here in his London studio with *Landscape with Church* (1957), a portrait and a nude. In 1959 Souza's *Words and Lines* was published, and from 1967 he lived in New York, returning to India shortly before his death.

31 **Alexander Weatherson** (b.1930)
1958

Weatherson was born in Nottinghamshire and finished his art education in London at the Royal Academy Schools and the Courtauld Institute. Victor Musgrave represented Weatherson at Gallery One from 1955, giving him his first solo exhibition in February 1958. At the time of Weatherson's Gallery One exhibition of 1961, which featured his work alongside that of Otto Nebel, John Russell wrote in *The Sunday Times* that 'Mr Alex Weatherson applies a nimble and hilarious intelligence to the advanced techniques of the day.' His paintings, collages and mixed media works were often influenced by music. Weatherson had exhibitions at the Institute of Contemporary Arts (1964) and the Arts Spectrum (held at Alexandra Palace in 1971 and photographed by Kar's pupil John Couzins). From 1968 to 1991, while living in France and London, he was Principal Lecturer in Fine Art at Leeds Polytechnic.

32 **Jack Clemente** (1926–74)
1960

Clemente was born in Novara, Italy, where he graduated with a degree in literature and philosophy. He studied painting at the Milan Brera Academy before moving to Paris in 1952. Clemente had his first one-man show in 1953 at the city's Galerie de la Muette and in the same year he exhibited at the Galleria Apollinaire in Milan. In 1957 his work was shown at the New Art Centre in London. Clemente painted in an abstract style, drawing inspiration from pre-historical and geological imagery. In the 1960s he abandoned oil paint and started to work with assemblages of 'non-art' objects. Kar photographed Clemente in his Paris studio using a Rolleiflex camera in natural light.

33 **Hussein Shariffe** (1934–2005)
1960

Sudanese-born Shariffe was educated at Victoria College in Alexandria, Egypt. In England he studied modern history at Fitzwilliam College, Cambridge, before joining the Slade School of Fine Art. His first solo exhibition of paintings, which included *Angel Pregnant with Moon*, opened at Gallery One in July 1959, at which time he appeared in the *Tatler* and was quoted as saying, 'I often try to paint a bad picture … but I hardly succeed.' Shariffe's paintings, with their vivid juxtapositions of colour, were shown in a second solo show at Gallery One in North Audley Street in April 1963, shortly before he returned to Sudan. There he worked as a lecturer at the School of Fine Arts, Khartoum (1964–6) and founded the literary and arts periodical *Twenty One* in 1965. Wishing to reach a wider audience, Shariffe turned to film-making in the 1970s and as Head of the Film Section of the Sudanese Department of Culture (1973–6) he directed his first film, *The Throwing of Fire* (1973). In

1976 Shariffe moved back to Britain, completing his second film, *Tigers are Better Looking*, in 1979. Shariffe lived in Cairo for the last decade of his life, writing his unfinished film script, *Letters from Abroad*.

34 **Keith Vaughan** (1912–77)
1960

Vaughan never received formal artistic training, but developed his talent while working in advertising for Unilever. His work was influenced by Cézanne, Matisse, Picasso and Gauguin, and the themes of landscape and the male nude dominated his paintings throughout his career. During the Second World War, unlike a number of his contemporaries who became war artists, Vaughan was a conscientious objector. The first exhibition of Vaughan's drawings was held in 1942 at the Reid and Lefèvre Gallery in London. During the 1940s and 1950s he taught at Camberwell School of Arts and Crafts, the Central School of Arts and Crafts and the Slade School of Fine Art. Predominantly a private artist, Vaughan received few public commissions, although recognition of his status in British art was shown by the commissioning of a mural for the Festival of Britain in 1951. Kar photographed Vaughan in his Hampstead flat when he was developing a looser and more abstract style, two years before his retrospective exhibition at the Whitechapel Art Gallery.

35 **John Kasmin** (b.1934)
1959

Kasmin was educated at Magdalen College School in Oxford before working at various jobs and writing poetry in New Zealand. On his return to England in 1956 he began to work as assistant to and promoter for Kar, often encouraging her to photograph writers whom he was eager to meet. Kasmin also assisted in the running of Gallery One. He wrote to Musgrave, 'the gallery has been very busy, rarely empty. Students, bores, painters and the odd leaven.' Kasmin opened his own gallery in 1963, with a Kenneth Noland exhibition and David Hockney became one of his first artists. Kasmin's focus was on abstraction and he exhibited British artists such as Anthony Caro and the Americans Frank Stella and Barnett Newman. The large white space on New Bond Street with a rubberised floor, designed by Ahrends, Burton and Koralek, was revolutionary at the time. Kasmin closed this gallery in 1972 but continued to represent his artists and in 1977 opened the Knoedler Kasmin Gallery, where he held an exhibition of Kar's vintage prints in 1982. Kar photographed Kasmin at his home, 18 Fouberts Place, London, after he had moved out of the D'Arblay Street building. On the fireplace are a Ben Nicholson relief (*c*.1930), African combs and a pre-Columbian pot.

36 **Bryan Robertson** (1925–2002)
1958

Robertson began his career as a junior sub-editor on *Studio* magazine, then worked for the Lefevre Gallery in London before his appointment as director of the Heffer Gallery in Cambridge.

His directorship of the Whitechapel Art Gallery (1952–68) resulted in a significant contribution to the visual arts in Britain. He revived the poorly funded gallery, staging ground-breaking exhibitions of past, established and emerging artists from Britain and further afield, including abstract expressionists from the USA, as well as promoting education through art. In 1958 he wrote to Kar to confirm previous discussions that she would have a large exhibition of her work at the gallery in 1960. His faith in Kar and her work was evident in the preface to *Ida Kar: An Exhibition of Artists and Writers in Great Britain, France and the Soviet Union*: 'She has brought out an intent sense of dedication in many of the sitters ... She is dedicated to life, to acceptance and to giving rather than taking.' Robertson's influential *New Generation* exhibitions began in 1964 with a group of pop painters including David Hockney.

37 **Erica Brausen** (1908–92)
1959

In the 1930s, German-born Brausen moved to Paris, where she mixed in the artistic circles of Montparnasse, before moving to London. She began her career in art dealing at the Redfern Gallery, before opening the Hanover Gallery in 1947 with the backing of the American banker and gallery owner Arthur Jeffress. For twenty-five years the gallery was hugely important in the international art world, hosting, for example, Francis Bacon's first solo exhibition (1949). As the gallery owner David Wolfers wrote for the *Tatler*, 'Continental sculpture has been an important feature – Marini, Manzu, Giacometti, Germaine Richier ... She has been a pioneer in making money out of sculpture and getting people to buy it for their homes.' Kar photographed Brausen with Germaine Richier's *La Tauromachie* (1953) at the Hanover Gallery. The photograph was published in 'A Gallery of Names that mean Galleries' in the 20 May 1959 issue of the *Tatler & Bystander*.

38 **Helen Lessore** (1907–94)
1959

Born in London into a Jewish family, Lessore studied at the Slade School of Art (1924–8). In 1931 she became secretary at the Beaux Arts Gallery, whose director was the sculptor Frederick Lessore. They married in 1934, and she took over the directorship upon his death in 1951. Helen Lessore commented that the fact she was an artist 'put me on the side of the artist, rather than of anyone else'. The *Tatler & Bystander* caption for a variant pose published in the story 'A Gallery of Names that mean Galleries' stated: 'Mrs Lessore hopes and believes that her artists will in time be considered the greatest in the country ... besides Bratby [his paintings can be seen in the background] she shows paintings by Middleditch, Michael Andrews, Frank Auerbach and Sheila Fell – realist painters all. Mrs Lessore comments: "I do not find abstract art satisfying."' Many of Lessore's artists gained distinguished reputations. The work of Walter Sickert, about which Lessore first wrote in 1932, was a constant at the Beaux Arts Gallery until its closure in 1965.

39 Cecil Beaton (1904–80)
1960
Beaton's interest in photography began as a young boy, when he was inspired by postcards showing actresses of the day. Through his friendships with Stephen Tennant and Osbert and Edith Sitwell, Beaton gained access to a wide range of innovative and creative subjects. In 1927 he signed his first contract with *Vogue*, with which he was associated throughout his life. During the Second World War Beaton served at the Ministry of Information, photographing in Britain, North Africa and East Asia. Of Beaton's post-war designs for the stage, film, ballet and opera, his most famous was the stage production of *My Fair Lady* (1956), the musical based on George Bernard Shaw's *Pygmalion*. Beaton won two Oscars for his work on the 1965 film version. He had been awarded his first Oscar for the costume design of *Gigi* (1958). Kar photographed Beaton in the conservatory of Reddish House, his Wiltshire home. The sitting produced various poses and Kar chose to enlarge the image of Beaton standing for her forthcoming Whitechapel exhibition. In a letter to Kar, Beaton wrote that the portraits of him were 'very good indeed'.

40 Bernard Kops (b.1926) **with his wife, Erica** (b.1934)**, and their son, Adam** (b.1956)
1960
Kops was born into a Jewish family in the East End of London, the setting for his first play *The Hamlet of Stepney Green* (1957). He ran a bookstall at Cambridge Circus (1953–7), not far from Gallery One at Litchfield Street, and became friends with Kar and Musgrave. Here Kar photographed Kops with his wife Erica (a scientist whom he had met in a coffee house and married in 1956) and son Adam (who later became a sculptor) in their Monmouth Street home. Colin MacInnes used the couple as models for characters Mannie and Miriam Katz in *Absolute Beginners* (1959). Kops returned to his childhood neighbourhood to review Kar's Whitechapel exhibition for the socialist *Tribune* newspaper, writing; 'Her artists are human no matter what … apart from being decorative, art can show people to people …' As well as subsequent plays, including *Ezra* (1981) and *Playing Sinatra* (1991), Kops has written poetry, most recently *This Room in the Sunlight* (2010), novels, an autobiography and scripts for radio and television.

41 John Bratby (1928–92) **with his wife, Jean Cooke** (1927–2008)**, and their son, David** (b.1956)
1959
Bratby was a prolific painter with a vigorous style who became associated with the avant-garde movement known as the new realism and with the kitchen-sink artists, who celebrated the everyday life of ordinary people. In 1954 his public career was launched with a solo exhibition at the Beaux Arts Gallery (his paintings can be seen in Kar's photograph of Helen Lessore (p.97), who named him 'the poet of the commonplace'). Bratby represented Britain at the 1956 Venice Biennale, and in 1957 was commissioned to paint the pictures for the film *The Horse's Mouth*, starring Alec Guinness. Bratby also wrote several novels,

including the autobiographical *Breakdown* (1960). He became a Royal Academician in 1971. Bratby married fellow painter Jean Cooke in 1953, and Kar photographed the couple with their son, David, at their house in Hardy Road, Blackheath. The couple painted each other on numerous occasions, and David also appeared in many of Bratby's domestic scenes. Kar's variant portrait of Bratby alone was used to publicise a Beaux Arts Gallery solo exhibition in the *Tatler & Bystander*. The accompanying caption stated that Bratby's hobby was 'collecting junk shop oddities'. An assured figurative painter, Cooke had her first solo show at the Leicester Galleries in 1964 and exhibited her work regularly from then on.

PORTRAITS OF WRITERS

42 Colin MacInnes (1914–76)
1957
The son of the singer James Campbell McInnes and the novelist Angela Thirkell (another of Kar's sitters), MacInnes spent his childhood in Australia, and, in the late 1940s, a period working in Germany, which inspired his first novel *To the Victors the Spoils* (1950). Back in London MacInnes first visited Gallery One at Litchfield Street as an art critic before renting a room in the D'Arblay Street building (1956–8), where Kar photographed him. Here, within Soho's 'two square miles of vice', MacInnes wrote *City of Spades* (1957), the first of his London novels, which empathetically depicted teenagers and black immigrants. MacInnes became a great friend of Musgrave and Kar and wrote in the foreword to the Whitechapel catalogue that 'an Ida Kar portrait is at once identifiable by its purity and distinction; she brings to each one an intuitive penetration and a thoroughly conscientious professional care.' Inspired by his friend Terry Taylor, who became Kar's assistant, MacInnes's novel *Absolute Beginners* (1959) stars a photographer. His biographer, Tony Gould, notes that 'the only predictable thing about Colin was his unpredictability', and as such his later works are as varied as a history of British music hall and historical novels.

43 Laurie Lee (1914–97)
1956
Lee spent his childhood in Gloucestershire, left school aged fifteen, and in 1934 moved to London, walking there with very little besides his violin. Lee wrote poetry while working as a labourer by day and spending his evenings in Soho cafés. He was an International Brigade volunteer in the Spanish Civil War, and during the Second World War worked as a journalist and scriptwriter. Lee decided to pursue his writing career after his poetry appeared in *Horizon* magazine (then edited by Cyril Connolly), publishing his first volume, *The Sun My Monument*, in 1944. Kar photographed Lee a year after the publication of *A Rose for Winter* (1955), an account of a period spent in Spain with his wife, Kathy Polge. The following year, the Hogarth Press paid Lee £500 to concentrate on writing his most acclaimed work, the autobiographical *Cider with Rosie* (1959). The success of this book

funded Lee's purchase of Rose Cottage in Slad, Gloucestershire, although he never gave up his Chelsea flat, the hub of his social life, where Kar photographed him against a backdrop of pin-ups. Lee's works *As I Walked Out One Midsummer Morning* (1969) and *A Moment of War* (1991) completed his autobiographical trilogy.

44 Doris Lessing (b.1919)
1958
Lessing was born in Iran and brought up in Zimbabwe. She left school aged fourteen and began to write. On her arrival in Britain in 1937, Lessing worked as a telephonist in Salisbury and married Frank Wisdom, with whom she had two children, but, feeling trapped, Lessing left her family in 1943. She married Gottfried Lessing after meeting him at the Left Book Club, moved to London with her young son in 1949, and published her debut novel *The Grass is Singing* in 1950. This photograph resulted from Kar's second portrait session with the author in her Earls Court flat, at the time in which Lessing was writing the novel quintet *Children of Violence* (1952–69). The stories, about a character called Martha Quest, are strongly influenced by Lessing's own rejection of a domestic role and her involvement with communism. Lessing's novel *The Golden Notebook* (1962) was heralded as an example of the new wave of feminism. With her novels in the 1970s she continued to write about the pressures of social conformity, before turning her attention to science fiction. Lessing was awarded the Nobel Prize for Literature in 2007.

45 Samuel Selvon (1923–94)
1956
Trinidad-born Selvon worked there in the late 1940s as a literary editor at the *Sunday Guardian* and as a journalist for the *Evening News*. He published several short stories and poems under pseudonyms before moving to London in 1950. His first novel, *A Brighter Sun* (1952), received international acclaim and established Selvon as an important voice at a time when London was becoming a centre for West Indian literature. Selvon's most celebrated novel, *The Lonely Londoners* (1956), was the first of three London novels narrated in the expressive and humorous dialect of his West Indian characters. His Trinidad novels, such as *Turn Again Tiger* (1958) and *The Plains of Caroni* (1970), portray Indians in Trinidad, who were then regarded as an ethnic minority. In the 1970s Selvon held a fellowship in creative writing at Dundee University before moving to Canada. In 1982 he became the first writer-in-residence at the University of the West Indies.

46 Iris Murdoch (1919–99)
1957
Murdoch moved from Dublin to London while still a child and was later educated at Badminton School, Bristol. She graduated with an outstanding first-class degree from Somerville College, Oxford (1942) and studied philosophy at Newnham College, Cambridge (1947–8), before becoming a tutor at St Anne's College, Oxford until 1963. Murdoch's first book, *Sartre: Romantic Rationalist*, was published in 1953 and was followed

by her debut novel, *Under the Net*, a year later. Kar photographed Murdoch as she worked on the manuscript for *The Bell* (1958), one of her most popular novels and the first to be influenced by Plato (a book on whom can be seen in the foreground). Kar photographed the writer at Cedar Lodge, Steeple Aston, where she had moved two years previously on marrying the author, critic and fellow Oxford don, John Bayley. Murdoch became best known for her novels about political and social questions of good and evil, sexual relationships, morality and the unconscious. Her subsequent novels included *A Severed Head* (1961), *The Unicorn* (1963) and the Booker Prize-winning *The Sea, The Sea* (1978). She was made a Dame in 1987.

47 Eugène Ionesco (1909–94)
1960
Romanian-born Ionesco grew up in France, returning to Bucharest in 1925. After obtaining a degree in French at the University of Bucharest, he studied for a doctorate in Paris, where he eventually settled. Ionesco's first play *La cantatrice chauve* (*The Bald Soprano*, 1949) revolutionised dramatic techniques and helped launch the Theatre of the Absurd. His avant-garde style dramatised the futility of social conventions and attacked totalitarianism and conformity. Along with Samuel Beckett and Jean Genet, who lived and worked in Paris during the same period, he remains one of the most important dramatists of the twentieth century. Ionesco was elected to the Académie Française in 1970. In Kar's portrait he appears at his writing desk. On the right hangs a poster for his play *Victimes du devoir* (*Victims of Duty*, 1953), and on his desk are copies of *The Possessed* by Fyodor Dostoevsky, in which Ionesco played the role of Stepan Trofimovich. At the time of the opening of Kar's Whitechapel exhibition, Ionesco's *Rhinocéros* (1959) was presented at the Royal Court Theatre, directed by Orson Welles.

48 Jean-Paul Sartre (1905–80)
1961
Sartre studied philosophy at the École Normale Supérieure and at the Sorbonne. From 1931 to 1945 he taught philosophy at Le Havre, Laon and Paris. His first novel, *La nausée* (*Nausea*), published in 1938, contained many of the existentialist ideas that he later developed. *L'Etre et le néant* (*Being and Nothingness*), Sartre's central philosophical work, was published in 1943. It defends individual freedom and human dignity. The concepts of freedom and social responsibility were also examined in *L'Existentialisme est un humanisme* (*Existentialism and Humanism*). During the Second World War Sartre was a member of the Resistance movement in Paris, and in 1946, together with the writer and philosopher Simone de Beauvoir, his lifelong partner, he founded the literary and political review *Les temps modernes* (*Modern Times*). He wrote many critically acclaimed plays, including *Les mouches* (*The Flies*, 1943). In his later years he was active in left-wing politics and wrote extensively about existentialism and Marxism. He was awarded the Nobel Prize for Literature in 1964, but declined it. Kar photographed Sartre

among stacks of books and manuscripts in his apartment on the boulevard Raspail in Montparnasse.

49 Helmut Gernsheim (1913–95)
1962

Gernsheim studied art history in his home town of Munich before taking up photography in 1934. Being part-Jewish, he used an offer of work to escape Nazi Germany and in 1937 moved to London. During the Second World War he photographed for the National Buildings Record and wrote his critique *New Photo Vision* (1942). Gernsheim began to collect work by early photographers including Julia Margaret Cameron and Lewis Carroll, and, along with his wife Alison, published *The History of Photography* (1955), a definitive study and one of seventeen volumes that the couple wrote between 1948 and 1966. Gernsheim sold his vast collection to the University of Texas in 1963. He was one of Kar's key champions and included her in his survey *Creative Photography: Aesthetic Trends 1839–1960*, as well as arranging for the acquisition of 124 prints for his collection in 1966. Writing for Kar's 1963 Birmingham exhibition, he noted: 'Today her work is gaining an international reputation and many people consider her to be one of the leading portrait photographers of famous contemporaries.' Kar photographed Gernsheim at his flat in Primrose Hill, north London, on 13 January 1962, with his collection of African art.

50 André Breton (1896–1966)
1960

The poet and critic Breton studied medicine and psychiatry before serving in the First World War. Through his friendship with Guillaume Apollinaire, Breton met Philippe Soupault, and, together with Louis Aragon, they co-founded the review *Littérature* (1919–24). In 1920 Breton and Soupault published *Les champs magnétiques* (*The Magnetic Fields*), the first example of the surrealist technique of automatic writing, influenced by Freud's analyses of the human unconscious. In 1924 Breton officially launched the surrealist movement with the publication of the first *Surrealist Manifesto*. He was editor of *La révolution surréaliste* from 1924 and helped organise the first surrealist group exhibition in 1925. Important publications include critical works, such as *Le surréalisme et le peinture* (*Surrealism and Painting*, 1926), and the novels *Nadja* (1933) and *L'Amour fou* (*Mad Love,* 1937). Kar photographed Breton at his Paris apartment-studio, 42 rue Fontaine, near Montmartre, where he lived with his third wife, Elisa. Breton moved to this address in 1922 and the flat served as the central office of surrealism. Breton is seen at his writing desk surrounded by the artefacts he collected. On the wall hangs one of Breton's most treasured paintings, Giorgio de Chirico's *The Child's Brain* (1914), and a portrait by Picasso.

51 Royston Ellis (b.1941)
1960

Ellis left school at the age of sixteen to become a writer. Influenced by the American Beat poets, Ellis's first book *Jiving to Gyp: A Sequence of Poems* (1959) chronicled life in Soho coffee shops and jazz clubs. In 1959, backed by Cliff Richard and the Drifters, Ellis appeared on various shows performing his 'rocketry', a mix of music and poetry that had been popularised by Jack Kerouac and others. During this time Ellis also performed with the young guitarist Jimmy Page, who was later to found Led Zeppelin. In 1960 the Beatles backed Ellis at the Jacaranda coffee bar in Liverpool. Ellis introduced John Lennon to 'Polythene Pam' in 1963; later she became the subject of a Beatles song. Ellis's book *The Big Beat Scene* (1961) was one of the first accounts of the contemporary music scene in Britain. Ellis currently lives in Sri Lanka, writing travel books and fiction.

52 Laura Del Rivo (b.1934)
1961

The writer Del Rivo grew up in Surrey. Her first novel, *The Furnished Room* (1961), set in bohemian London of the 1950s, was successfully adapted in 1963 as the film *West 11*. Del Rivo took over the writer Colin Wilson's Notting Hill flat in 1956, and since the 1960s she has run a stall at Portobello Market. She published some of her early work in *Intimate Review,* an underground paper edited by the poet John Rety. The paper circulated among the literary crowd of the Soho coffee houses and attracted contributions from many contemporary writers, such as Doris Lessing, Bill Hopkins and Bernard Kops. Kar met and photographed Del Rivo at Peter Russell's bookshop, which occupied the ground floor of 20 D'Arblay Street, just beneath Gallery One, where Del Rivo worked at this time. During this period Del Rivo also published *Daffodil on the Pavement* (1867) and *Animals* (1970).

53 T.S. Eliot (1888–1965)
1959

Missouri-born Eliot settled in England before the First World War. While working in Lloyd's Bank he published collections of verse, *Prufrock and Other Observations* (1917) and *Poems* (1919), hand-printed at the Hogarth Press by Leonard and Virginia Woolf. Eliot founded the literary magazine *The Criterion* in 1922, publishing *The Waste Land* in the first issue. In 1925 he joined the staff of the publishing house Faber & Faber, and established a reputation for promoting younger writers, including W.H. Auden and Stephen Spender. Eliot's later work included *Murder in the Cathedral* (1935) and *Four Quartets* (1935–42). He was awarded the Nobel Prize for Literature in 1948. This was Kar's second sitting with Eliot, at the offices of Faber & Faber in London.

54 Somerset Maugham (1874–1965)
1958

Maugham qualified as a doctor in 1897, but pursued his passion for writing following the publication of his first novel, *Liza of Lambeth*, in the same year. His play *Lady Frederick*, staged at the Royal Court in 1907, was his first theatrical success, and his largely autobiographical novel *Of Human Bondage* (1915) became a best-seller. It was followed by other highly praised works, such as *The*

Moon and Sixpence (1919), the satirical *Cakes and Ale* (1930) and *The Razor's Edge* (1945). Numerous successful adaptations were derived from Maugham's short stories, including *Quartet* (1948) and the Alfred Hitchcock film *The Secret Agent* (1936). Kar photographed Maugham at the Dorchester hotel on a visit to London from his home on the French Riviera. By this time he had gained a reputation as a grand old man of letters, known for his sparse, careful prose. His essays on Goethe, Chekhov, Henry James and Katherine Mansfield were published in *Points of View* in the year this photograph was taken.

LE QUARTIER ST IVES

55 Barbara Hepworth (1903–75)
1961
Yorkshire-born Hepworth studied at Leeds School of Art and at the Royal College of Art, along with her friend Henry Moore. In 1924 she was awarded a travel scholarship to Italy, where she married the sculptor John Skeaping. Hepworth joined the avant-garde Seven and Five Society in 1931 and was a member of other groups of artists, including Abstraction-Création and Unit One. Ben Nicholson became her second husband in 1938, and the following year she moved with him to St Ives in Cornwall. Although the marriage was dissolved in 1951, their mutual influence persisted, and both achieved international recognition in the post-war period. Hepworth's global standing was confirmed when she was awarded the Grand Prix at the 1959 São Paolo Bienal, followed by the second of two Whitechapel exhibitions in 1962. A commission for the *Tatler* allowed Kar to photograph the sculptor. Hepworth is seen here at work on the armature of a sculpture at the Palais de Dans, a former cinema and dance hall which she acquired to serve as an additional workshop and store. This portrait was exhibited for the first time in Kar's 1962 Moscow exhibition. Hepworth was made a Dame in 1965.

56 Patrick Heron (1920–99)
1961
Heron was born in Leeds, but spent much of his childhood in Cornwall. In the late 1930s he studied part-time at the Slade School of Art in London. As a conscientious objector during the Second World War, Heron worked as an agricultural labourer and then at the Leach Pottery, St Ives. In 1956 he bought a home in Zennor, Cornwall, called Eagles Nest, where his family had lived for a time in the late 1920s. The house and its surroundings became a centre for artists and writers in St Ives and central to all Heron's future work. From that time he moved away from figurative painting in favour of abstraction, becoming a member of the Penwith Society in 1952. In 1945 and 1946 Heron wrote reviews for the *New English Weekly*, and was art critic for the *New Statesman and Nation* (1947–54). He also wrote about art education and fought to stop the military taking over the West Penwith landscape. Among his most influential written works is *The Changing Forms of Art*, published in 1955, the year in which his work became predominantly abstract. Kar also photographed

Heron along with his wife, Delia, and daughters, Katharine and Susanna, at Eagles Nest for the *Tatler*.

57 John Milne (1931–78)
1961
Milne studied electrical engineering at Salford Royal Technical College but transferred to the Art School in 1951 to study sculpture and painting. After briefly studying at the Académie de la Grande Chaumière in Paris, and making the first of what would become regular visits to Greece, Milne moved to St Ives. He became the pupil of, and later assistant to, Barbara Hepworth, with whom he established a close friendship. Milne's early work was directly carved in stone, but from 1966 he started experimenting with metals and learned cold-casting methods for bronze and aluminium. His later work was influenced by the landscape and architecture of Greece. Kar photographed Milne at Trewyn, his St Ives home, which had a garden adjoined to Hepworth's studio. A close-up portrait of Milne holding one of his hand-carved sculptures, *The Kiss*, was the pose chosen for publication in the *Tatler*.

58 Terry Frost (1915–2003)
1961
Frost left school at fourteen and did not begin painting until he became a prisoner-of-war in Germany during the Second World War. After the War, Frost, with his wife, Kathleen, and the first of their six children, relocated to St Ives, living in a caravan at Carbis Bay before moving to a cottage in Quay Street, where Kar later photographed him. Although he studied at Leonard Fuller's St Ives School of Painting, the artistic community was equally important in the development of his abstract style, as were his studies at Camberwell School of Art in London (1947–9). Between 1952 and 1954 he was the pupil of, and later assistant to, Barbara Hepworth, and became a member of the Penwith Society of Arts. During this period he mounted his first solo exhibition at the Leicester Galleries in London and exhibited in Patrick Heron's *Space in Colour* show at the Hanover Gallery. Kar photographed Frost, looking out at 'the sun, glittering water and boats' which influenced his work, in the year after his first solo show in New York, where he met and was inspired by American abstract artists. Frost was knighted in 1998.

59 Peter Lanyon (1918–64) with his daughter, Anne-Marie
1961
The St Ives-born sculptor Lanyon trained at the Penzance School of Art in Cornwall and briefly attended the Euston Road School in London. His work was greatly inspired by Ben Nicholson, Barbara Hepworth and the Russian constructivist sculptor Naum Gabo, with whom he established a close friendship. Lanyon served with the Royal Air Force during the Second World War, after which he became actively involved with the modernist Crypt Group and the Penwith Society of Arts. During the 1950s he was a leading figure in the St Ives group of artists, establishing his international reputation with a solo exhibition in New York in

1957. Kar photographed Lanyon with his daughter, Anne-Marie, in the garden of their home at Little Park Owles, Carbis Bay, outside St Ives, which Lanyon had acquired in 1954. Formerly the home of Adrian Stoke, the house was an important centre of artistic activity, sheltering Ben Nicholson and Barbara Hepworth during the Second World War.

DOCUMENTARY PORTRAITS

60 State lottery, Stalinstadt
1959
Kar travelled to East Germany in September 1959, ten years after the formation of the German Democratic Republic (GDR). An exhibition of her Armenian photographs was held in Berlin at the Zentrale Haus der Deutsch–Sowjetischen Freundschaft (Central House of German–Soviet Friendship) and Kar took reportage photographs in both black-and-white and colour. She recorded state nannies with a group of children and young Thälmann Pioneers – members of a socialist, Scout-like organisation – at camp. In Stalinstadt, founded in 1950 as the first new German town built after the Second World War, Kar documented the life of the Schillers, a typical East German family, and in her scribbled notes commented that, despite having two jobs, they had never had a holiday. Elsewhere in the city Kar captured the dashed hopes of a woman by a state lottery stand. The German state lottery was founded in 1938 and Kar wrote on the back of this photograph that, at the time, a fifty-pfennig ticket could win you a cash prize of 400,000 deutschmarks.

61 Boys at the indoor market, Yerevan
1957
Kar returned to Armenia in 1957, both to fulfil a commission and to visit her ageing parents, whom she had not seen for ten years. She was treated as an honoured guest and, thanks to her fluency in Russian and Armenian, her comfortable base at the Hotel Armenia and her government driver, she enjoyed a productive visit. Her Armenian album contains contact prints of artists and peasant workers, public monuments and ruins. Eleven photographs made during this Armenian trip were shown in the Whitechapel exhibition, including a portrait of a monk, a silhouette titled *Study of a Radar* and a portrait of her father. The two boys posing for Kar inside the covered market in Yerevan are seen among soldiers in Russian uniform, which, Kar noted, stood to remind 'loungers on the steps of the collective market that this is the USSR' (Armenia remained under Soviet rule until 1991). In her *Tatler* cover story, 'Return to Armenia', Kar added, 'I still carry with me a picture of the hot colours and shimmering towers and peaks of my country, and my pride at belonging to such a warm-hearted nation.'

62 Juan Arcocha (1927–2010), Havana
1964
Arcocha studied law, journalism and languages at university. During the 1960s he was foreign correspondent in Moscow for the Cuban newspaper *Revolución* and later worked in the press

office of the Cuban Embassy in France. Arcocha was interpreter to Jean-Paul Sartre and Simone de Beauvoir during their visit to Havana in 1960. His command of languages also allowed him to work for international organisations such as the United Nations. In 1966, disillusioned with the restrictions imposed on artists by the Cuban regime, Arcocha moved to France. He wrote numerous novels, the last of which was published in May 2010, just a few days before he died.

63 Hugo Consuegra (1929–2003) with his wife, Rita Arias, Havana
1964
Havana-born Consuegra trained at the city's San Alejandro Academy of Arts and went on to gain a degree in architecture from Havana University. His first solo exhibition was held in 1953 at the Lyceum, Havana, and in 1954 he became one of the founding members of Los Once (The Eleven), a group of young painters and sculptors who introduced abstract expressionism to Cuba. He had numerous group and solo shows across the United States and Europe, winning several awards, and was professor of art history at Havana University's School of Architecture (1960–5). In 1967 Consuegra went to Madrid, where he lived for three years before moving to New York. He became an American citizen in 1975. Kar photographed Consuegra and his wife, Rita Arias, at the artist's studio in Havana, posing between canvases.

64 Alberto Korda (1928–2001), Havana
1964
Korda was born Alberto Díaz Gutiérrez in Havana. He formed Korda Studios in partnership with Luis Pierce (also photographed by Kar) in 1956. This portrait is part of a series of photographs Kar took of Fidel Castro's friend and official photographer. He appears in front of a mural commemorating the 26th of July Movement which, led by Castro, succeeded in overthrowing General Fulgencio Batista's regime in 1959. Korda is best known for his portrait of Ernesto 'Che' Guevara, *Guerrillero Heroico* (1960), which, since the late 1960s, has become one of the most iconic images of revolution and protest.

65 *Taking a Breeze in Old Havana*
1964
Ida Kar's Cuban photographs are considered the best photo-journalism of her career. In an article entitled 'Ida Kar: Reborn in Cuba', published in the 19 January 1964 issue of the Cuban newspaper *Hoy*, the journalist Marta Vignier wrote of Kar's fascination for the revolution and of the enthusiasm with which she embraced her job as a photographer, documenting life in Havana and the surrounding countryside. This portrait of a young woman with her baby was taken in Havana as Kar wandered the city's streets. It was included in the exhibition *Ida Kar in Cuba*, held at Hamiltons Gallery, London and Stepney Central Library, east London, in 1965. The critic Peggy Delius, writing in the *British Journal of Photography* (12 February 1965), noted: 'Taking a breeze in old Havana has a rare quality of

pathos, and to me personally that of a lingering beauty. Clearly the observer was observed by the young woman as this remarkable picture came into being.'

THE LONDON SCENE AND LATER SITTINGS

66 **Maggie Smith** (b.1934)
1961
Smith was born in Ilford, east London, and studied acting at the Oxford Playhouse School. She appeared in revue in the 1950s before joining the Old Vic Theatre (1959–60). Her work in Jean Anouilh's *The Rehearsal* (1961) and in Peter Shaffer's comedies *The Private Ear* and *The Public Eye* (both 1962) solidified her reputation. She joined the National Theatre Company in 1963, most notably playing Desdemona in *Othello* opposite Laurence Olivier. Smith made her film debut in *Nowhere to Go* (1958), followed by important cameos in films such as *The V.I.P.s* (1963) and *The Pumpkin Eater* (1964). Her starring role in *The Prime of Miss Jean Brodie* (1969) earned her an Oscar for best actress. A major star since then, Smith's performances in *California Suite* (1978), *A Room with a View* (1985), *Gosford Park* (2001) and the film adaptations of J.K. Rowling's *Harry Potter* series have confirmed her status as a leading British actress. She was made a Dame in 1990. Kar photographed Smith in the role of Lucile, on the set of *The Rehearsal*.

67 **Terry Taylor** (b. 1933)
1961
Taylor studied art before working as an actor and photographer. He was introduced to Musgrave and Kar in the late 1950s by Colin MacInnes, and from then worked as Kar's assistant for two years. He recalls that 'Gallery One was a hub of creative activity'. Encouraged by MacInnes, Taylor wrote the novel *Barons Court, All Change* (1961), for which Kar's photograph was reproduced as the frontispiece. Taylor's interest in jazz is reflected in a number of portraits made at the same time taken in Soho and in his Knightsbridge flat. He remembers, 'Anyone who was familiar with Ida's work saw that she was not just a photographer, but an artist. How she incorporated the sitter's working environment was unequalled … she had a wonderfully natural personality that enabled the sitter to relax.'

68 **Brian Robins** (1928–88) **with his wife, Susan**
1960
Welsh-born Robins left school aged fourteen and worked at various manual jobs. When he met Kar and Musgrave in the early 1950s, he was working as the last lamplighter in London. Robins was self-taught as a sculptor and his work was exhibited at Gallery One in 1954. A year later he photographed Kar with his carved wooden portrait of her (a version of this image was used on the cover of Kar's Whitechapel exhibition catalogue). Robins exhibited alongside the painter Ralph Rumney at the New Vision Centre (1956) and became noted for his kinetic sculptures, shown in a solo exhibition at the Grosvenor Gallery (1966). This

photograph shows Robins and his wife Susan at The Farm, their short-lived basement coffee shop at 14 Monmouth Street in Covent Garden, which became a meeting-place for young artists and poets after the couple opened it on 23 June 1959. As well as selling coffee, its aim, according to Robins, 'was to show works which the commercial galleries would not show … I felt that art freed from the purse strings would give it more scope and personality.' Robins showed work by Gustav Metzger, Roger Mitchell and Susan Bryan. The last exhibit before the closure of The Farm in May 1960 was Robins' painting machine, which produced a picture every twenty minutes.

69 **Bridget Riley** (b.1931)
1963
Riley studied at Goldsmiths' College of Art (1949–52) and the Royal College of Art (1952–5). A leading exponent of op art in Britain, Riley worked initially in black-and-white, introducing full colour in 1967. Riley's first solo exhibition was held at Gallery One in 1962 and in 1964 she was the only woman to be included in *The New Generation* at the Whitechapel Art Gallery. A series of overseas shows in 1964 further boosted her reputation and she won the International Prize for Painting at the 1968 Venice Biennale. Her meticulously executed paintings have powerful and subtle perceptual effects and express what Riley has termed 'the pleasures of sight'. Kar photographed Riley at her second exhibition at Gallery One, 16 North Audley Street, London in September 1963. This was the final show before Musgrave closed the Gallery.

70 **Gustav Metzger** (b.1926)
1962
Born to Polish-Jewish parents in Nuremberg, Metzger came to Britain with his brother in 1939, under the auspices of the Refugee Children's Movement. Metzger exhibited with the Borough Bottega (an art group centred on his former teacher David Bomberg) in 1953, and his first solo exhibition, of paintings on galvanised steel, was held at Brian Robins' coffee shop The Farm in 1959. Metzger became dissatisfied with painting and began to theorise about 'auto-destructive' art. From 1960 Metzger was a member of the Committee of 100 and Kar photographed him making anti-nuclear protest pieces by applying acid to sheets of nylon. She photographed him the following year walking through London with a bag of rubbish, as part of the first public demonstration of auto-destructive art. Here he is shown outside Gallery One's exhibition *Festival of Misfits* by the Dada-influenced Fluxus Group (which was also held at the Institute of Contemporary Arts). Metzger's contribution, comprising the front page of the *Daily Mirror* covering the Vietnam War, was rejected and removed by other participants. Metzger has continued his career making politically challenging pieces and an extensive exhibition of his work was held at the Serpentine Gallery in 2009.

71 **John Latham** (1921–2006)
1963
John Latham studied at Chelsea School of Art (1946–50) and had his first solo exhibition at the Institute of Contemporary Arts in 1960. He became a pioneer of conceptual art in Britain, working in a variety of media including spray paint and, later, assemblage incorporating plaster and books. During his time teaching at St Martin's School of Art (1966–7) he and a group of students chewed pages of Clement Greenberg's book *Art and Culture*. A phial of the resulting material was titled *Spit and Chew: Art and Culture*. In 1966, with his wife Barbara Steveni, Latham formed the Artist Placement Group, an initiative that aimed to place artists in government, commerce and industry. Latham was photographed by Kar shortly before his exhibition, *Latham's Noit*, at the Kasmin Gallery, London.

72 **Oskar Rabine** (b.1928) **with his wife, Valentina Kropivnitskaya** (1924–2008)**, and their son, Alexandre** (1952–94)
1962
Rabine trained with the Russian painter and poet Evgeny Kropivnitsky. He went on to study at the Riga Academy of Arts before returning to his native Moscow to continue his training at the Surikov State Art Institute, from which he was expelled for non-conformism. In 1950 Rabine married Valentina Kropivnitskaya, his teacher's daughter, and settled in Lianozov, Moscow, where their son, Alexandre, was born. Rabine was a founding member of the Lianozovo Group that brought together non-conformist artists whose art did not follow the official socialist-realist style. Banned from exhibiting by the Soviet authorities, he was the first unofficial Soviet artist to have a solo show in the West (at the Grosvenor Gallery, London, in 1964). In 1978 Rabine was forced into exile in France, where he continues to live and work. Kar photographed Rabine and his family at their home in Lianozov when she travelled to the USSR to attend the opening of her exhibition in Moscow.

73 **Paul Millichip** (b.1929) **with his wife, Felicity Evershed, and their children, Diana and Robin**
1960
Millichip studied at Leeds College of Art and Brighton College of Art. He had his first solo exhibition at Gallery One in January 1955 while still a young painter living in Brighton, and his work continued to be exhibited in the gallery throughout the 1950s, often alongside other artists such as F.N. Souza and John Christoforou. Millichip was recommended to Victor Musgrave, at the then recently opened Gallery One, by Peter Gimpel of Gimpel Fils Gallery. This photograph was taken just outside the studio room at Millichip's West Hampstead flat before a solo show at Gallery One. The works in this photograph were all included in the exhibition and were concerned with figures in movement, both singly and in groups. Millichip remembers: 'Ida Kar was an Armenian of very positive temperament and outlook – fiercely aware of her abilities and talent.' Here he is photographed alongside his first wife, the artist Felicity Evershed, and their children, Diana and Robin, as well as the family's Siamese cat, Mr Greibson.

74 **Bill Brandt** (1904–83)
1968
Brandt was born in Hamburg and learned photography in a Viennese studio in the 1920s, before spending three months in 1930 as an assistant to Man Ray at the height of the surrealist movement. Brandt settled with his wife Eva in London in 1934 and published his first photographic impressions of the country as *The English at Home* (1936), followed by *A Night in London* (1938). Brandt's commissions for *Lilliput* magazine from 1941 established him as a portraitist, and he became a regular contributor to *Harper's Bazaar* in the 1950s and 1960s. A series of portraits of writers was published as *Literary Britain* in 1951. In 1944 Brandt began to photograph nudes with a large wide-angled police camera. The photographs, showing the influence of Matisse and Henry Moore, were published in *Perspective of Nudes* (1961), which was followed by a career survey, *Shadow of Light*, in 1966. Kar, with her assistant John Couzins, photographed Brandt in his flat in Airlie Gardens, Kensington (in some of the portraits Brandt's second wife, Marjorie Becket, can just be seen). The year after this photograph was taken, Brandt was honoured with a retrospective exhibition at the Museum of Modern Art, New York (1969) and the Hayward Gallery, London (1970), which brought Brandt to the attention of a new generation. Brandt shared Kar's approach in that he said, 'I always take portraits in my sitter's own surroundings.'

75 **Mother and child**
1974
In the summer of 1974 Kar embarked on what was to be her last photographic project. In her bedsit at 47 Inverness Terrace, Bayswater, she erected a makeshift studio and took several intimate portraits. Here a pregnant woman poses with a child. The contact sheets from this session of 22 August show how the cherished portrait of Kar's father, included in her Whitechapel exhibition, was removed from its hook for the duration of the session. Kar clearly intended several of her nudes for public display, as she had ordered enlargements of the retouched images; they were delivered to her shortly before her death in December.

SELECT BIBLIOGRAPHY

Clarke, Graham, *The Photograph: A Visual and Cultural History* (Oxford: Oxford University Press, 1997)

Garlake, Margaret, *New Art/New World: British Art in Postwar Society* (New Haven: Yale University Press, 1998)

Gernsheim, Helmut, *A Concise History of Photography* (London: Thames & Hudson, 1971)

Gernsheim, Helmut, *Creative Photography: Aesthetic Trends 1939–1960* (London: Faber & Faber, 1962)

Gould, Tony, *Inside Outsider: The Life and Times of Colin MacInnes* (London: Chatto & Windus, 1983)

Grunenberg, Christoph and Harris, Jonathan (eds), *Summer of Love: Psychedelic Art, Social Crisis and Counterculture in the 1960s* (Liverpool: Liverpool University Press, 2005)

Harrison, Martin, *Transition: The London Art Scene in the Fifties* (London: Merrell, 2002)

Kinley, Monika, *Monika's Story: A Personal History of the Musgrave Kinley Outsider Collection* (London: Musgrave Kinley Outsider Trust, 2005)

Rideal, Liz, et al., *Mirror, Mirror: Self-Portraits by Women Artists* (London: National Portrait Gallery, 2001)

Rogers, Malcolm, *Camera Portraits* (London: National Portrait Gallery, 1989)

Rosemont, *Penelope, Surrealist Women: An International Anthology* (Austin: University of Texas Press, 1998)

Rosenblum, Naomi, *A History of Women Photographers* (New York: Abbeville Press, 2000)

Wedd, Kit, et al., *Artists' London: Holbein to Hirst* (London: Merrell, 2001)

Williams, Val, *Ida Kar: Photographer 1908–1974* (London: Virago Press, 1989)

Williams, Val, *Women Photographers: The Other Observers 1900 to the Present* (London: Virago Press, 1986)

PICTURE CREDITS

ACKNOWLEDGEMENTS

Ida Kar was one of the first names I heard when I began work at the National Portrait Gallery as Assistant Curator of Photographs in 2000. She was not a photographer I had heard of before, but I soon became familiar with Kar's work as I was given the task of cataloguing a large part of her archive, which the Gallery had acquired the previous year. For this fascinating assignment I would like to thank the Curator of Photographs, Terence Pepper, who has inspired and guided the project over the last ten years. In the Photographs Collection, I would especially like to thank Georgia Atienza, who has worked alongside me over the last few months in preparing the visual and written material for this publication and the exhibition. Georgia has also been invaluable in the organisation and cataloguing of the Ida Kar archive. I am most grateful to Val Williams, the author of the only previous Kar monograph, who has been key to the assembly of information surrounding the photographer's work and life. I should also like to thank Monika Kinley, through whom the Gallery acquired the archive and who had been a good custodian of Kar's work.

In the preparation of this book, and the exhibition it accompanies, I have been indebted to a number of people who shared with me their first-hand knowledge of Ida Kar. The literary photographer Mark Gerson, a friend of Kar's for the whole span of her time in London, has been involved with the project from the outset. John Kasmin has provided invaluable insights into Kar's world in the late 1950s and has generously given his time to identify sitters who might have otherwise been overlooked in Kar's oeuvre. Julie Green (previously known as Julieta Preston) recounted vivid stories of her time as Ida Kar's assistant. John Couzins, another of Kar's assistants, sadly died in July 2009. His brother Martin made sure that we were given access to John's collection. Through this the Bill Brandt negatives came to light, as well as further information about the later years of Kar's life. Martin Couzins has also generously lent some original material for the exhibition. Martin Breese, another of Kar's assistants, fortuitously got in touch through the National Portrait Gallery website. Some of Kar's sitters were most helpful with adding context and vibrancy to our understanding of the portraits: I would like to thank John Hitchens (son of Ivon), Bernard and Adam Kops, Paul Millichip, Laura Del Rivo and Bridget Riley.

Stewart Home was a very helpful source of information regarding Terry Taylor, another of Kar's close acquaintances, and the bohemian culture that surrounded him. He put me in touch with Taylor himself, who in turn was able to provide further first-hand information about Kar. I also contacted John Cox, who told me much about about Kar's friend Brian Robins. Caroline Worthington and Jennifer Gray helped in the identification of sitters and sculptures in the large number of negatives relating to Jacob Epstein and the Garman family. Don Chapman at Camera Press, who remembered Kar visiting the premises on numerous occasions, was very kind in identifying which of her portraits had been syndicated to the world's press by the agency. Robin Bell and Norman Kent took great care in the printing of Kar's negatives.

This project has involved numerous people from many departments of the National Portrait Gallery. I am grateful to our Director, Sandy Nairne, for recognising the value of an exhibition of Ida Kar's portraits. I would especially like to thank Rosie Wilson in the Exhibitions Department as well as Sarah Tinsley and Michelle Greaves for their help and encouragement over the last three years; Celia Joicey, Head of Publications; Robert Davies, the editor of this catalogue; Denise Ellitson, Head of Marketing; Neil Evans in the press office; Liz Dewar in the Digital Programmes Department; and Ian Gardner and Natalia Calvocoressi for the exhibition design. Further thanks to Anisa Hawes, Camilla Sutherland, Inga Fraser, Amanda Hajjar, Imogen Lyons, John Riley, Krzysztof Adamiec and Grace Keeble for assisting with research as well as the continued support of my colleagues in the Photographs Department.

Clare Freestone, November 2010

158

INDEX